yoga

a *flow***motion**™ title

yoga

liz lark

BARNES & NOBLE
BOOKS
NEW YORK

Created and conceived by
Axis Publishing Limited
8c Accommodation Road
London NW11 8ED
www.axispublishing.co.uk

Creative Director: Siân Keogh
Managing Editor: Matthew Harvey
Project Designer: Anna Knight
Project Editor: Michael Spilling
Production Manager: Sue Bayliss
Photographer: Mike Good

Library of Congress Cataloging-in-Publication
Data Available

10 9 8 7 6 5 4 3 2 1

First Barnes & Noble edition published in 2004
Published in 2002 by Sterling Publishing Co., Inc.
387 Park Avenue South, New York, NY 10016

Separation by United Graphics Pte Limited
Printed and bound by Star Standard (Pte) Limited

Sterling ISBN 0–7607–5670–8

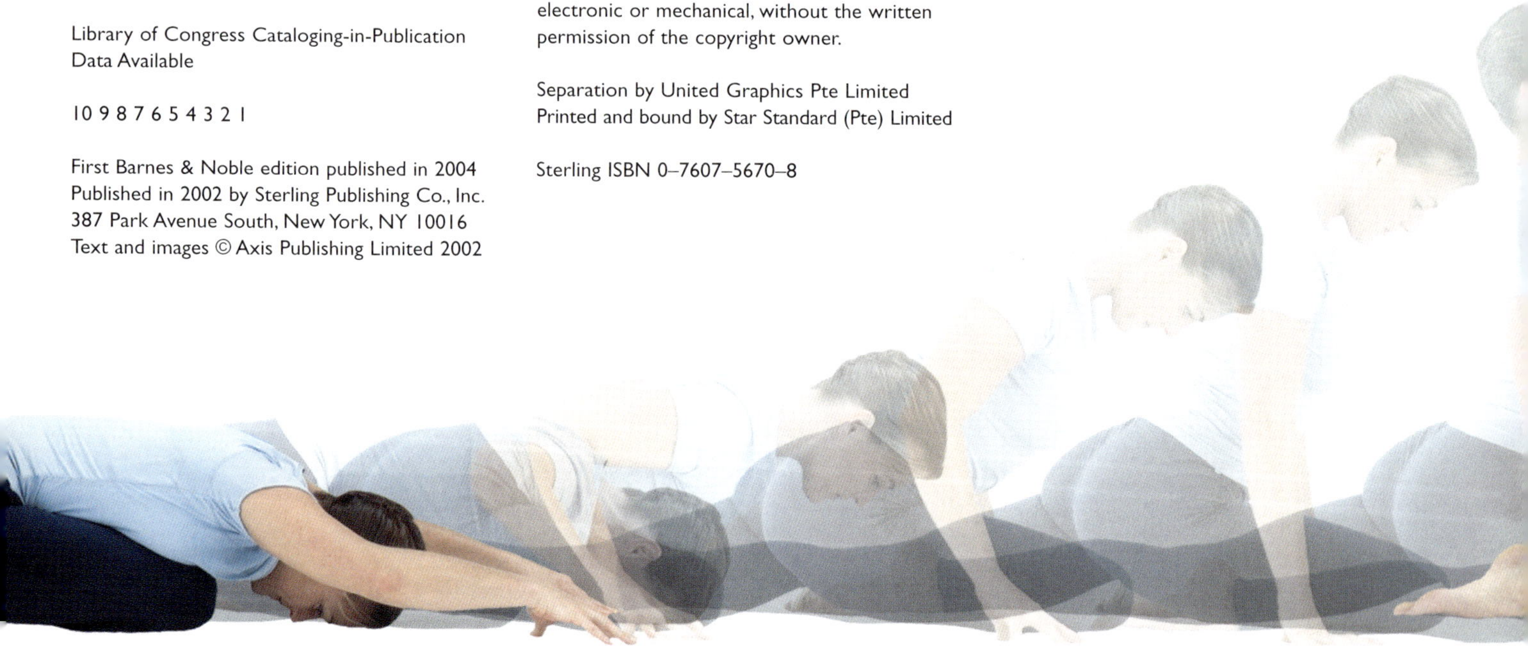

a *flowmotion*™ title

yoga

contents

introduction

"Only that day dawns to which we are awake."

HENRY DAVID THOREAU, *WALDEN*

Over 5,000 years ago, the seers and Rishis (forest dwellers), who inhabited the Indus Valley in northern India, practiced the ancient art of yoga. Through observing their own bodies and minds, they developed postures and breathing exercises to raise mental awareness and bring about meditative states where the mind becomes likened to "a sea without waves."

The Rishis practiced techniques that became crystallized between 400 B.C. and A.D. 400 in the verbally transmitted *Yoga Sutra* of the sage Patanjali. Yoga means "to yolk," or "union," while sutra means "thread." The second sutra of Patanjali defines yoga as, "the stilling of the thought waves of the mind." Patanjali's *Yoga Sutra* offers an eight-limbed ascending path to raise consciousness through yoga practice. This book follows the techniques and teachings of Patanjali.

yoking the mind—drawing in its reins

The mind has been described as a chariot pulled by wild horses that toss it this way and that. The object of yoga practice is to tame these wild horses and train them through observation. In this book we will practice hatha yoga, a type of yoga that offers a tangible path by combining movement with breathing techniques to grasp the mind and bring it home. Today, there is a rising wave of interest in yoga and meditation: both practices help to create a healthy, strong, illness-resistant body, and soothe and calm the mind,

enabling us to access silence. There is a desire in the human soul to journey and to seek retreat and simplicity. In the West, this mood became prominent in the 1960s and reawakened with the new century, perhaps as a reaction to materialist culture, which has sacrificed the essence and spirit of the individual in favor of material gain.

It is said that yoga offers a path that helps us remember who we are. The heart of yoga is meditation, wherein the mind sits without distraction or disturbance in the present moment. Scientists estimate that an average person has around 50,000 thoughts each day, most of which serve only to avoid the opportunity of living in, and appreciating, the present moment.

"Don't leave your house to the see flowers,
My friend, don't bother with that journey.
Inside you there are flowers.
Each flower has a thousands petals
That will make a place to sit."

KABIR

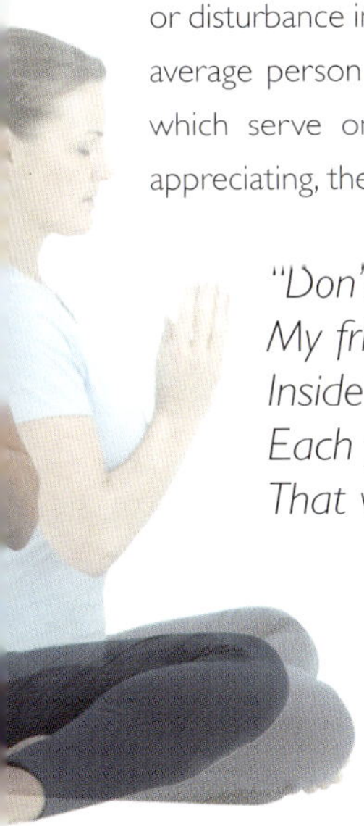

SIDDHASANA Achieving effective meditation is the ultimate goal of yoga practice, and many advanced students practice meditation.

STYLES OF YOGA

Historically, there are five main styles of yoga, all of which share the same goal: union, or stilling of mind.

JNANA

The path of wisdom, emphasizing self-inquiry and discrimination through intellectual knowledge.

HATHA

The path of mind control that uses Patanjali's eight-limbed tree of yoga. The aim is to balance sun (ha) and moon (tha) energy.

BHAKTI

The path of devotion through surrendering the heart to a spiritual discipline. Saints and mystics of all religions follow this path.

KARMA

The path of action, which serves (and reflects) unconditionally one's selfless actions and behavior.

RAJA

The path of kings combines karma, jnana, and bhakti yoga in a contemplative method that uses the body as a vehicle for spiritual energy.

Patanjali's hatha yoga: the tree of eight limbs

In much of the developed world today, the most commonly practiced and perhaps the most accessible form of yoga is hatha yoga, an umbrella term used to denote the styles of yoga that utilize the eight limbs outlined by Patanjali. Hatha yoga emphasizes balancing the opposing forces in the body, such as masculine energy (the sun), feminine energy (the moon), left and right, and inhalation and exhalation, restoring the body to its natural equilibrium. Consequently, hatha yoga practice often involves movements that alternately move the body in two opposing directions.

In Pada 2, Sutra 29 of the *Yoga Sutra*, Patanjali identifies the eight limbs of hatha yoga. These provide an ascending pathway to the liberation of the mind. The first two limbs consist of moral and social guidelines, in order that people live well as individuals and collectively. The other limbs deal with various elements of yoga practice. Limbs three and four in particular provide the basis of hatha yoga.

HAND POSITIONS

Some yoga *asanas*—especially those that involve meditation—require the hands to be held in specific gestures, called *mudras*. *Mudras* are thought to guide the energy flow and are an integral part of yoga posture. *Namaste*, the prayer pose, involves holding the palms of the hands flat together. *Ynana*, the seal of wisdom, involves linking the index finger and thumb together, symbolizing receptivity and calm. Cupping the hands in the *Dhyani mudra* is also popular for meditation.

NAMASTE—PRAYER POSITION

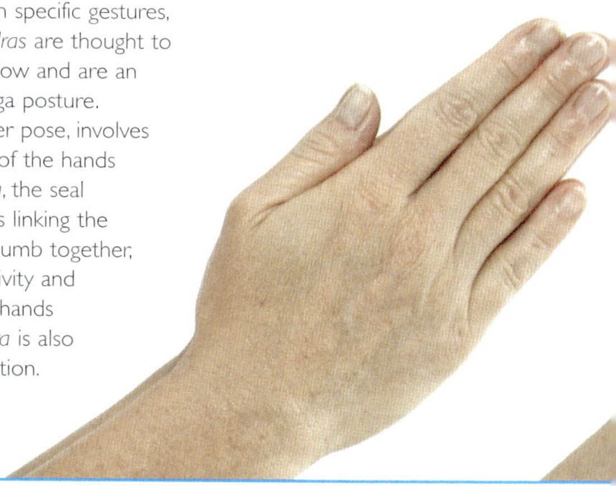

1. YAMA: THE FIVE OBSERVANCES

These are restraints or rules of conduct. They include *ahimsa* (non-violence, epitomized in the life of Mahatma Gandhi), *satya* (truthfulness), *asteye* (non-stealing), *brahmacharya* (control of the vital, sexual energy), and *agarigraha* (non-possessiveness).

2. NIYAMA: THE FIVE ACTIONS

The five actions include *saucha* (inner and outer purification), *santosha* (contentment), *tapas* (discipline), *swadhaya* (reading of spiritual books), and *Ishwara pranadhanini* (surrender to the god of nature—Ishwara is the lord of nature).

3. ASANA: TO SIT IN STEADINESS

The importance of *asana*, or correct posture, is twofold: first, it increases physical wellbeing with a set of integrated physical exercises; second, *asana* is a preparatory stage and foundation for the practice of yoga, which is of the mind. *Asana* is the first conscious step on the path of yoga, creating a strong person.

4. PRANAYAMA: THE SCIENCE OF BREATHING

In yoga, *prana* is cosmic energy (a subtle, creative life-force); so *pranayama* means the control and cultivation of the vital energy in the body, which is contained in the inward and outward breaths.

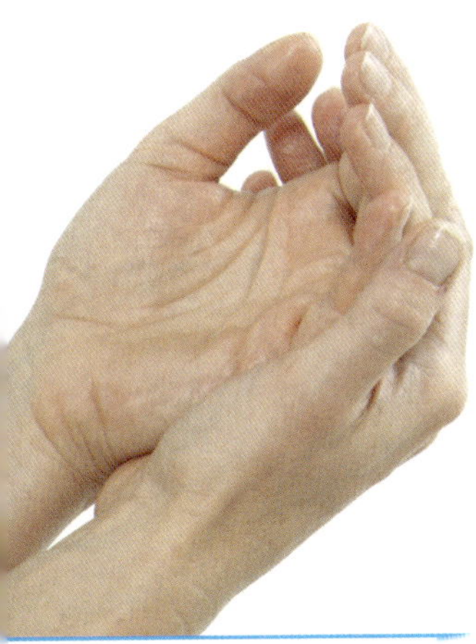

DHYANI – CONTEMPLATION

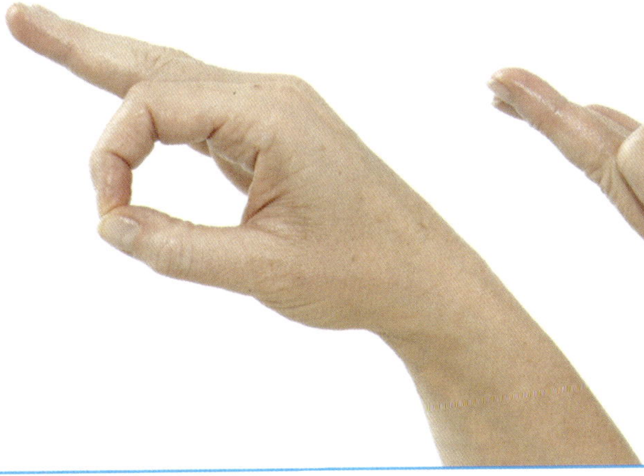

YNANA—SEAL OF WISDOM

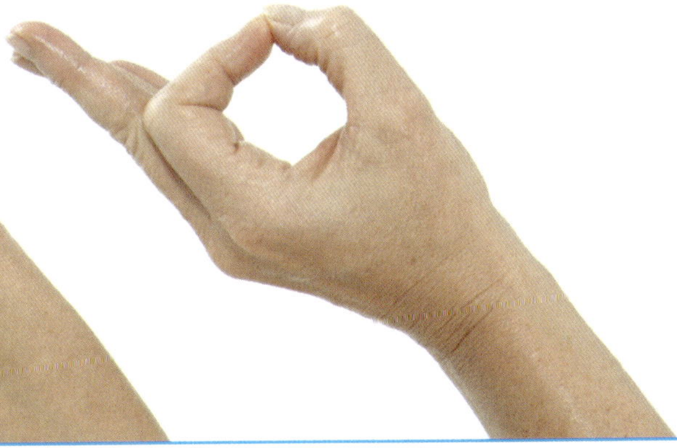

YNANA—SEAL OF WISDOM

5. PRATYAHARA: WITHDRAWAL OF THE SENSES

Pratyahara—withdrawal of the senses from the outer world to awaken the senses of the inner world—leads the student from the external practices of yoga to the essential internal aspects. These include inner focus, concentration, and meditation.

6. DHARANA: CONCENTRATION

This is the ability to focus the mind on an object without faltering. The lower limbs have prepared the mind for concentration, drawing the focus inward to release the ties that bind the person to the physical world.

7. DHYANA: MEDITATION

When the concentrated mind becomes absorbed in the object of focus, a meditative state is attained. In meditation, which is the heart of yoga, every moment is a special moment. As the German writer J.W. von Goethe said, "Be attentive to the present. Only in the present time can we understand eternity."

8. SAMADHI: BLISS, UNITY, AND TRANSCENDENCE

Mind mastery is attained when one is absorbed in meditation, thus transcending the limitations of time and space. One has moved, in yogic terms, from the limitations of the small ego-driven self, to the liberation of the soul-orientated Self. *Samadhi* is a culmination of the seven lower limbs and the ultimate goal of yoga.

preparing for practice

"Find a quiet retreat for the practice of yoga, sheltered from the wind, level and clean, free from rubbish, smoldering fires, and ugliness, and where the sound of water and beauty of the place help thought and contemplation."

SVETASVATARA UPANISHAD

The ancient texts recommend a peaceful environment where one is connected to nature and oneself. However, today most yoga sessions are taught in classes, although traditionally yoga was passed down on a one-to-one basis. It is important to learn from a qualified, experienced teacher who can monitor your practice and confirm that a posture is safe for your level. This book offers a safe, gradual, supportive approach to basic yoga.

Here we include some warm-ups—Arm Stretches, Neck Roll, Shoulder Shrugs, and Side-to-Side—and gentle breathing awareness (see pages 16–17). There is no need for any other preparatory exercises. What is important is to prepare yourself for practice by creating a calm environment where you can concentrate in peace: switch off the telephone, close the door, clear your mind of worries; and then begin.

Correct breathing is the key to obtaining mastery of the mind. Breathing with awareness allows us to capture moments, so always be aware of your breathing. Breathing awareness must continue unhindered throughout the practice even if postures become a little difficult.

SHOULDER SHRUGS To loosen up the shoulder joints, sit upright in the mediation pose with your legs crossed and your hands resting on your knees. Now gently shrug your shoulders up toward your ears, then drop them again. Repeat the exercises three or four times.

diet and lifestyle

Without the correct diet and lifestyle, performing yoga *asanas* will not be of great benefit, although it is often by practicing that one begins to change other lifestyle habits. The ancient yogis realized that diet had a profound effect on mind and body, so they classified foods into three categories, which are encompassed in the *gunas*, or qualities, that make up the universe:

TAMAS (over-ripe): Tamasic foods are those that are impure, stale, processed, or loaded with additives. They drain the resources of the body rather than replenish them.

RAJAS (under-ripe): Rajasic foods are stimulating foods that lead to emotional surges, but in the long-term are not beneficial. They include spicy, bitter, pungent foods, and include concentrated forms of protein (such as meat and eggs), coffee, alcohol, and excessive sugars.

SATTVA (succulent): Sattvic foods are those that are perfectly ripe and fresh, vital, fragrant, and tasty. They include foods that are natural, organic, and fresh, such as fruits, vegetables, nuts, and seeds. These foods help clear thinking and boost our contemplative and intellectual faculties, increasing health and energy. Yoga practice seeks to attain the sattvic quality in all things.

One is advised to eat, as in yoga practice, in a calm, quiet environment, in order to assimilate and digest food well. Three meals a day, or even two, are adequate. Most of all, enjoy the food!

NECK ROLL Before starting any yoga routine, loosen your neck and shoulder joints. Sit in the meditation pose and roll your head in a smooth 360-degree circle. This will loosen the muscles and increase blood circulation.

"The unmoved is the source of all movement."

LAU TSU, *TAO TE CHING*

three-part breathing

Dirga pranayama—the three-part breath—involves actively breathing into three different parts of your abdomen. These are the lower belly (just below the belly button), the lower chest (lower ribcage), and the lower throat (just above the sternum).

1

1 Begin the first breathing position with your knees raised, feet rested flat on the floor, and hands resting at your sides. Begin breathing from the lower belly, slowly inhaling. Place your hands on your lower belly and feel the breath.

2 Now progress to the second position, breathing deeply from the lower chest. Place your hands on your lower ribcage and feel the breath rise and fall.

2

● You may want to start practicing by isolating the movement in each position using your hands. When you have a good feel for the breath moving in and out of each position, practice without the hands. Eventually, relax the effort of the *pranayama* and breathe into the three positions gently, feeling a wave of breath move up and down your torso.

3

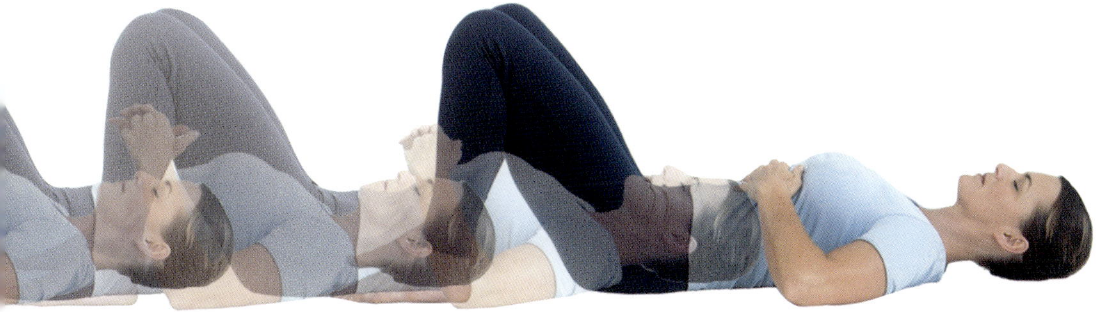

3 In the third position, let your breath rise up to your throat. Move your hands to rest on your throat and feel the breath passing through. Repeat the sequence three or four times, breathing deeply from the belly up to the throat.

yoga for all

Yoga is for everyone. The 20th-century master Krishnamacharya said that as long as one can breathe, one can practice yoga: it is a misconception to believe that yoga is for certain types of people. Yoga is inclusive, not exclusive, and can be practiced by anyone, regardless of their culture or religion. Yoga has many uses: for sport people, the *asanas* correct and tone the body and improve alignment. The practice cultivates body awareness, helps rebalance the left and right sides, improves movement, conserves energy by engaging the correct muscles, and relaxes those that are not necessary for a movement. Yoga is also a good way of beating stress. For performers and speakers, the practice develops controlled use of breathing and heightened focus and concentration. It also helps develop self-confidence and self-empowerment. Yoga can make life extraordinary in opening up creative channels by removing muddy layers of perception and negative thought processes.

ARM STRETCHES It is important to perform this movement before beginning a yoga session. Sitting in the meditation position with legs crossed (see pages 118–119), make the spine alert by drawing your shoulders back.

- Draw your hands over your head and link your fingers together with the palms facing up. Extend your arms as far as you can. This will stretch your arms, shoulders, and back. Hold the stretch for a few breaths.

It important to find a teacher who will encourage and guide you to practice appropriately and safely according to your needs and abilities. As people, we are always changing, and yoga practice should develop organically, too. Practice should never be dogmatic: thus with every breath, try to practice anew the beginners' state of mind.

Finally, remember that the essence of yoga is the liberation of the mind. Think about this carefully, and do not let your attention wander. In yoga we explore inwardly to find balance rather than outwardly in the chaos of the world around us. Yoga values the unseen and the invisible, looking with the inner eye of discernment rather than the conditioned outer eye.

THE BENEFITS OF YOGA

The soothing and benevolent teachings of yoga have multifarious benefits, ranging from the physical and visible to the subtle and spiritual. Swami Pragyamurti, a Satyananda Yoga monk, said that yoga allows us "to live as we want to, usefully, lovingly, and interestingly."

- **realigns the body, strengthening bones and joints, and tones and lengthens muscles**
- **builds self-esteem and self-acceptance**
- **detoxifies the system, purifying the internal system**
- **builds strength, flexibility, and stamina**
- **increases blood circulation, which improves respiration and raises energy and vitality**
- **calms the mind and soothes the emotions, removing anxiety**
- **brings focus and clarity**
- **massages the internal organs, thus improving bodily functions**

using the Flowmotion method

FlowMotion is suitable for complete beginners, providing a safe introduction that begins with supine postures and works through warm-up *asanas* toward the more advanced standing postures. The method is progressive, and no preliminary exercises are necessary. One should follow the sequence in its entirety. You should approach the practice with the two qualities of "zeal" (enthusiasm) and "surrender" (letting go), as laid down by Patanjali (*Yoga Sutra*, Pada 1, sutras 22 and 23). Practicing with effortless effort creates a meditative state, flowing naturally from the breathing.

SIDE TO SIDE
To loosen the neck muscles, move your head from side to side in a smooth, gentle movement. Repeat three or four times.

REMEMBER THE FOLLOWING:

- Prepare a space that is warm, private, clean, and conducive to a calm mind.
- Wear comfortable clothing that allows you to move freely, preferably natural fibers. Practice in bare feet, but do not let them get cold.
- Only begin yoga practice two or three hours after eating; the stomach should be empty. If necessary, drink a glass of juice an hour before.
- Take a warm bath before practice: this can help loosen and warm stiff joints or muscles as well as cleanse your body.
- Consult your doctor before doing yoga if you have had recent surgery or illness.
- Do not begin a new program if you are pregnant: consult a specialized teacher for an appropriate class.
- Practice regularly. Daily practice is ideal—a little but often is best. Aim for 20 minutes a day, or three sessions a week at first. The benefits will make you wish to continue.
- Practice on a rubber yoga mat, thick enough to protect the spine and give a good grip for the feet in standing postures.
- Keep breathing constant and smooth. Do not hold the breath at all.
- Avoid strain or force in postures. There is no competition in yoga, and there is no end to a posture, just continuous observation and stretching.
- Relax at the end of the practice. You should be warm and comfortable—place a towel over the eyes, a blanket over the body, and socks on the feet.

go with the flow

The special *Flowmotion* images used in this book have been created to ensure that you see the whole of each *asana* – not just selected highlights. Each of the image sequences flow across the page from left to right, demonstrating how the *asana* progresses and how to get into each position safely and effectively. Each *asana* is labelled as being suitable for beginners, intermediate or advanced students by a coloured tab above then title. The captions along the bottom of the images provide additional information to help you perform the *asanas* confidently. Below this, another layer of information is contained in the timeline, including instructions for breathing and symbols indicating when to hold a position.

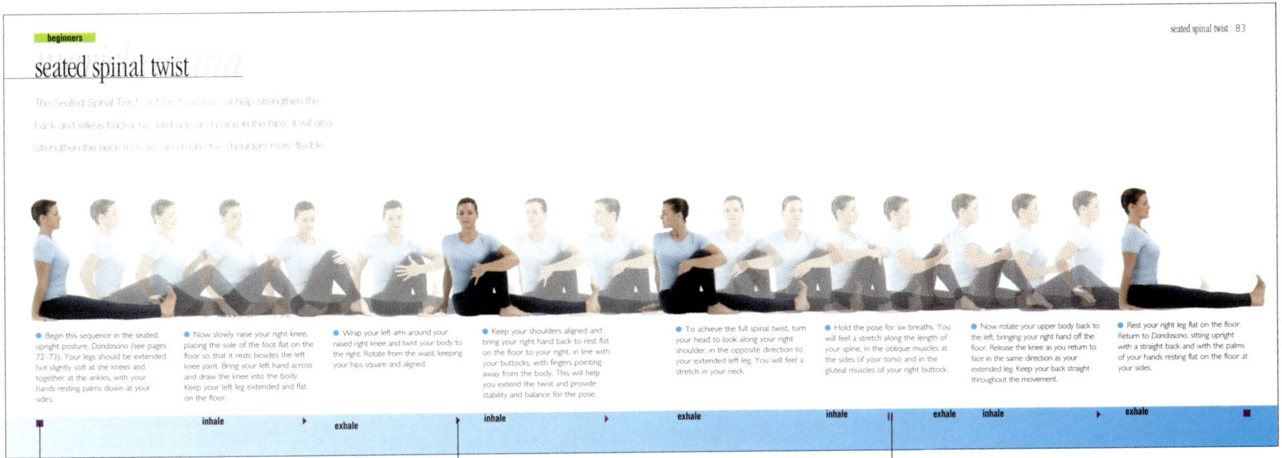

■ This indicates the beginning or end of a sequence, where there is no movement.

▶ This indicates continued movement in the sequence.

‖ This indicates a pause, either to hold a pose, stretch or take a number of breaths.

waking the body from the floor

preparing to curl

To gain the maximum benefit from yoga *asanas*, your body needs to be well aligned and centered. This exercise will strengthen your lumbar muscles and increase your spinal flexibility. It is a good preparation for Gas Ejector (pages 24–25) and Supine Twist (pages 26–27).

- Begin the pose by lying on your back with your arms extended above your head and resting flat on the ground. Make sure that your back is not arched away from the ground. Your legs should be outstretched with your feet pointing forward.

exhale

- Now bend your left knee and raise your foot off the floor. Clasp your hands together, with fingers interlaced, and swing your arms over your head toward your knee in a smooth, flowing movement, keeping your arms soft at the elbows.

inhale

- Interlace your fingers and hold your shin just below the knee. Inhale and gently pull the knee into the chest, but avoid pressing straight into the ribcage, as this can inhibit correct breathing.

exhale

- Keep your shoulders, head, and resting leg pressed flat against the floor and your hips square throughout the movement. Relax and hold the pose for three to six breaths.

- To come out of the pose, exhale and release the knee. Bring your arms forward, unlink your fingers, and slowly part your hands in a single flowing movement.
- Lower your arms toward the floor and slowly extend your leg back down to the starting position.
- Continue to lower the leg and bring your arms back to your sides. Rest your hands on the floor with palms facing up. Relax your body as you fully recline.
- Relax, with your legs extended and arms rested by your sides. Check that your back is not arching and keep your feet pointing forward. Repeat the movement using the other leg.

exhale ▶ **inhale** **exhale** ▶ ■

gas ejector

pavanmuktasana

This exercise will help improve digestion and remove any inner tension by massaging the internal organs. It will also increase spinal flexibility, stretch the lower back, and loosen the hips. This *asana* can also be practiced in a standing position (see pages 56–57).

- Approach this *asana* with caution if you suffer from neck problems. Begin the pose by lying on your back with your arms extended above your head and resting flat on the ground.

- Now raise your left knee back toward your chest. Link your fingers together and swing your arms toward your knee in a smooth, flowing movement, keeping your arms soft at the elbows. Bring your hands together and hold your shin just below the knee.

- Gently pull the knee into the chest using both arms, but avoid pressing hard into the ribcage. Keep your resting leg relaxed with toes pointed straight and your hips square. Hold the pose for three to six breaths.

- Come out of the pose by releasing the knee and slowly extending your leg back into the starting position. Lower the arms slowly and let them rest at your sides. Repeat the move using the other leg.

inhale **exhale** **exhale** **inhale**

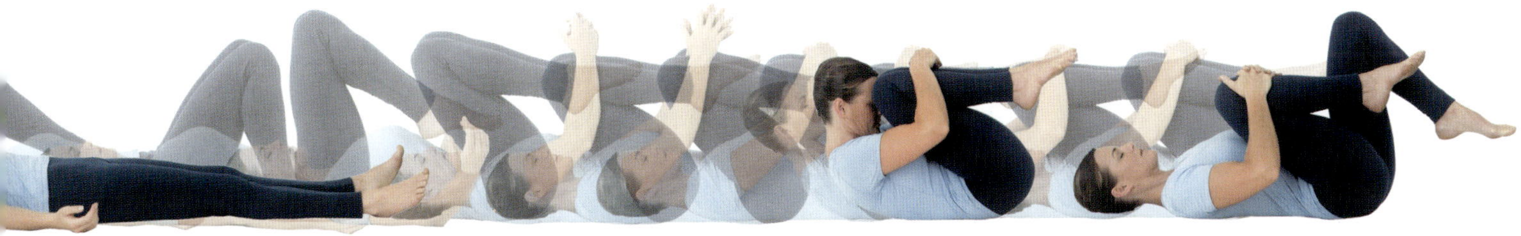

● Still lying on the floor, raise and bend your knees, keeping the soles of your feet flat on the floor. Now slowly bring both knees up toward your head and into the chest.

● Bring both arms forward to hug your knees tightly so your tailbone is lifted from the floor. Keep your head on the floor. Hold for three to six breaths. You will feel a stretch along your spine and in the hips.

● Now exhale and release the knees. From the raised position, repeat the knee squeeze with the right leg. Gently pull the knee into the chest using both arms, but avoid pressing hard into the ribcage.

● When you have finished, rest your head flat on the floor and relax your shoulders. Repeat the sequence two or three times.

exhale **inhale** II **exhale** **exhale** ▶ **inhale** II

supine twist

jathara parivartanasana

This *asana* opens out the chest and helps to promote relaxation. It will loosen and stretch the back muscles, and realign and lengthen the spine by hydrating the spinal disks.

- Do not practice this *asana* if you have recently suffered chronic injury to the knees, hips, or back. Begin the exercise lying on your back with your legs extended and ankles together.

- Now bring your right knee up to your chest. Link your fingers together and swing your arms toward your knee in a smooth, flowing movement, keeping your arms soft at the elbows.

exhale

- Interlace your fingers just below the knee and gently pull the knee into the chest using both arms. Now gently rotate your right knee to the left, using your left arm to to pull the knee down to the left.

inhale

- Exhale and push the knee down to the floor, twisting from the hips. This maneuver will twist the spine and lower back. Relax into the posture and use your left hand to hold the knee in position. Keep your extended leg straight and engaged.

exhale

● Stretch your right arm out along the floor, with finger tips extended. This will keep your shoulders flat on the floor and insure a correct stretch. Turn your head to the right, close your eyes, and relax. Hold the pose and take four or five deep breaths.

● Now inhale and push your right leg back to the center, rotating your body to bring your whole back to rest flat on the floor. Bring your left arm up and interlace your fingers and grip the shin, just below the knee.

● Now raise your left leg and pull the knee back toward the chest and in line with your right knee.

● Bring both arms forward and hug your knees tightly, keeping your back flat on the floor. Hold for three to six breaths. This will help reflow the spinal fluid and realign the vertebrae after the twist.

II **inhale** ▶ **exhale** ▶ **inhale** ▶ **exhale** II

intermediate

balasana

extended child into raised child

This sequence will enhance your flexibility and strengthen, and extend your spine, shoulders, and back muscles. Beginning in a relaxed Extended Child *asana* (also see pages 100–101), the movement progresses to a kneeling chest expander with extended arms. The kneeling chest expander stretches the neck intensely, so do not attempt it if your suffer from neck problems.

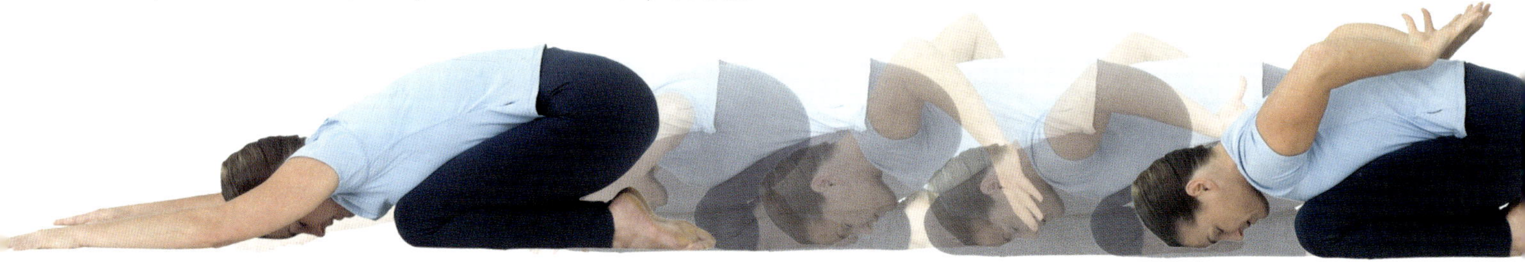

- Begin the sequence in the Extended Child *asana*, kneeling with your knees tucked under your body and your forehead resting on the floor. Your arms should be fully extended but relaxed, with the palms facing down.

inhale

- Your shins and feet should be flat against the floor, with your buttocks about an inch above your heels. Keeping your forehead rested on the floor, slide your hands back toward your body, lifting your elbows from the floor as you do.

exhale

- Gradually raise your arms behind your back and join your hands by interlacing your fingers. Keep your forehead rested flat on the floor throughout this movement.

inhale

- Lift your clasped hands and slowly extend your arms to lock at the elbows. Remember to keep your shoulders aligned – do not hunch them up toward your ears.

exhale

- Pushing from the knees, slowly raise your hips from the kneeling position. Keep your arms straight and fully extended throughout the raise. This will help maneuver your arms into the correct position for the full extension.

- Simultaneously, lift your head and gently roll it forward so the crown rests flat on the floor and your nose is pointing toward your knees.

- Fully extend your arms upright to 90 degrees into the Raised Child *asana*. You will feel a stretch between your shoulder blades and down your spine. Hold for three to six breaths, making sure you breath deeply into the belly and chest.

- To come out of the position, release the stretch and lower your arms back toward the floor and raise your head to sit upright. Unlink your fingers and bring your arms down and parallel to your body. Relax and sit with your spine straight.

inhale ▸ **exhale** ▸ **inhale** ▸ **exhale** II

intermediate

kneeling back bend

This movement provides a counterpose to the Raised Child *asana*. It is important to do these poses in sequence in order to realign the vertebrae and stretch the spine in both directions.

- Begin the back bend in the Raised Child *asana* (see page 29) – on your knees with your back arched and the crown of your head resting flat on the floor, with arms fully extended upright to 90 degrees, locked at the elbows, and hands clasped together.

- Release the stretch and lower your arms back toward the floor. Unlink your fingers and bring your arms down and in line with your body.

- Gently raise your upper body, hinging from the waist and keeping your back straight. Slowly roll your head upward until you are sitting fully upright, on your haunches, with your back straight and your arms relaxed at your sides.

- Hinging from the hips, gently recline your back toward the floor. Simultaneously move your arms behind to provide support, first balancing on your fingertips.

II **inhale** ▸ **exhale** ▸ **inhale** ▸ **exhale** ▸

- Walk your fingers back and away from the body until they are roughly eight inches away from your toes. This will help you achieve a greater back bend.

- Continue to lower your body backward until the palms of your hands are resting flat on the floor. Your fingers should be pointing forward, roughly in the direction of your body.

- Once your body weight is fully supported by your arms, push your chest outward and gently roll your head backward to point your chin at the sky. Hold the pose for three to six breaths.

- Continue to thrust your chest upward while reclining your head back as far as it will go without causing discomfort. Hold the pose for three breaths, then relax and return to the upright seated position.

exhale ▸ **inhale** ▸ **begin to exhale** ▸ **exhale** ||

cat *marjariasana*

The Cat *asana* is a basic yoga posture that will help flatten the stomach, strengthen the back muscles, improve spinal flexibility, and relieve lower back tension. Practiced every day, this exercise can greatly increase spinal mobility.

- Begin the exercise on your hands and knees. Place your hands flat on the floor in line with your shoulders, with your fingers spread apart and pointing forward. Keep a straight back and face down toward the floor.
- Slowly raise your head to face forward. At the same time, inhale and push your chest down and extend your tailbone up. Keep your hips square and your knees firm to maintain a steady posture.
- Drop your stomach toward the floor and face up. This will create a gently inverted arch in the spine. Relax and hold the pose for three to six breaths.
- Now release the stretch. Exhale and lower your head so that you are again looking down.

▶ inhale ▶ exhale II inhale exhale ▶

- Shuffle your hands in toward your body—this will help you achieve a more pronounced arch. Tuck your chin into your chest, drop your shoulders, and lower your tailbone.
- Exhale and raise your back vertically as far as your can, as if a string tied around your waist is pulling you up. This will create a gentle arch in the spine.
- Relax and hold the pose for three to six breaths. Keep your hands and knees firmly on the floor to maintain a good posture. Now relax your spine and return to the start position.
- Repeat the sequence two or three times. You can also practice controlling your abdominal muscles by contracting them and holding your breath when your back is arched up.

inhale ▶ ▶ **exhale** **inhale** ‖ **exhale** ▶ ■

intermediate

cat with raised leg

marjarisana

This exercise will help strengthen the hip joints, shoulders, and upper back and improve balance. Do not attempt this movement if you suffer from problems in your lower back.

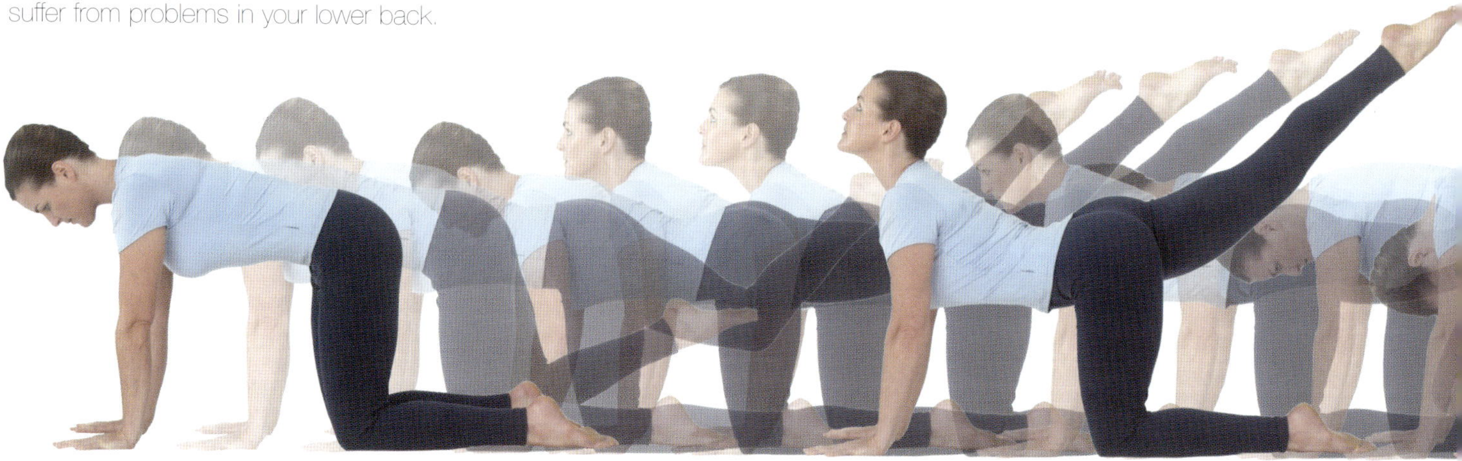

● Begin the exercise in the Cat *asana*. Kneel forward and place your hands flat on the floor in line with your shoulders, with your fingers spread apart and facing forward. Look down at the floor.

● Now, slowly lift your right knee from the floor, keeping your foot pointed backward. As you begin to extend your leg, slowly raise your head to face forward. Keep your hips aligned and do not twist them.

● Fully extend your right leg in a smooth flowing movement and point your foot at a 45-degree angle. With your head raised, your back should be slightly inverted. Hold this pose for four or five breaths. You will feel a stretch in your back and hamstrings.

● Then counterbalance this pose by arching your back upward. Return to the starting position by bringing your leg back down to the floor. Bring your right leg through and under your chest so your knee is in line with your extended arms.

■ exhale ▶ inhale II exhale inhale ▶

● Rest your forehead on your right knee to fully arch your back. This creates a stretch in the spine. Hold this pose for three to six breaths.

● Now, raise your head and bring your right leg back under your body to the Cat *asana*. Slowly lift your left knee and begin to raise your head.

● Repeat the move with the left leg. Fully extend the leg while slowly raising your head to face up. At the same time, lift your foot to point at 45 degrees in a single, smooth flowing movement.

● The pose should create a gentle curve from your head to the tip of your toes. Hold this pose for five breaths, then relax and return to the Cat *asana*.

exhale II **inhale** ▸ **exhale** **inhale** ▸ II

intermediate

cobra into twisting cobra

Practicing *Bhujangasana* will strengthen the abdomen, the arms, and the body core while deeply opening the chest, stretching the lower back, and improving oxygen intake. The turning of the head will make the neck muscles stronger and more flexible.

- Do not practice this *asana* if you have recently suffered injuries to your knees, back, arms, or shoulders. Begin the sequence kneeling on all fours in the Cat *asana* (see page 32).

- Now slowly bend your arms at the elbows and lower your head forward, toward the floor. At the same time, lift your tailbone, keeping your back straight. As you lean forward, your arms will take your body weight.

- Continue to push forward, bringing your hips down to the floor while bearing your upper body weight with your arms. Now inhale and in one smooth, flowing motion, lift your chest off the floor.

- Press your pubic bone down into the floor while extending your arms to keep your body steady. The lifting motion should come from pressing your pelvis and legs into the floor. Bring your head and neck up, and slowly roll your head backward.

inhale ▶ **exhale** ▶ **inhale** ▶

● With elbows tucked into your sides, press down into the palms and use your arms to gain a greater raise. Throw your head backward and arch your spine so your chin is pointing up. Hold the pose for as long as it feels comfortable.

● Now drop the shoulders and face your head forward. Keep your legs and buttocks strong, and keep the pubic bone pressing down into the floor. Use your arms to maintain balance. This position will continue to stretch your spine.

● Holding the position, twist your head to the left to face 90 degrees from the body. Hold for a few breaths. Now repeat the twist to the right.

● Release the pose. Exhale, lift your hips from the floor, and sit back on to your haunches to bring your legs under your body. Simultaneously lower your chest forward, extend your arms, and rest your head on the floor in the Extended Child *asana* (see page 28).

exhale ▶ **inhale** II **inhale** ▶ **exhale and rest** II

intermediate

downward dog

adho mukha svanasana

This *asana* will stretch the backs of your legs, open out the chest, massage the abdominal muscles, and increase circulation to the head and face. The Downward Dog is an important *asana* to master, as it is a key posture from which many sequences begin.

- Begin this movement as you finished the Cobra sequence (see page 37), in the Extended Child *asana*—kneeling back on your haunches with your arms outstretched and palms facing down. Rest your forehead against the floor.
- Slowly raise your body from the floor, pushing your hips forward and straightening your arms to move into the Cat *asana*. You should now be on all fours with your head facing down.
- Lifting from the toes, bring your tailbone up to straighten your legs to lock at the knees. Press your chest down toward the floor. Lock your elbows and drop your head between your arms to align with your back, facing toward your toes.
- Press the soles of your feet and the palms of your hands flat on the floor. Your body should form an inverted V shape. Hold the pose for three to six breaths. You will feel a stretch along the spine and around the buttocks in the gluteus maximus muscles.

■ inhale ▸ exhale ▸ inhale ‖ exhale

Release the pose by lifting your right knee out from under your body. Bring the knee forward toward your chest, maintaining balance on your left foot and keeping your hips square. Keep the palms of your hands pressed flat to maintain balance.

Let your hips drop toward the floor and bring your right knee as far forward as you find comfortable. The upper part of the right foot should be allowed to rest on the floor.

Now gently lower your chest toward the floor, bearing the weight with your arms. Rest your chest on your thigh and tuck your foot under your body. Stretch your extended leg fully with the toe pointing back.

Fully extend your arms along the floor, with palms resting flat and fingers pointing forward. Rest your forehead flat on the floor to take up the Extended Swan *asana*. Relax and hold the pose for six breaths.

inhale ▶ ▶ **exhale** **inhale** ▶ **exhale** ‖

intermediate

rajakapotasana

swan arch into downward dog

This sequence moves from Extended Swan to Swan Arch and finishes in the Downward Dog posture. These *asanas* will open out the chest, stretch the lower spine, and loosen the hips. They can be quite challenging and you shouldn't attempt them until you have established a good level of flexibility. Be sure to perform them slowly and steadily and don't rush through any particular section.

- Approach this *asana* with caution if you suffer from lower back problems. Begin the exercise in the Extended Swan pose, with your right knee tucked under your body, your left leg extended, and your arms fully stretched out in front of you.

- Now slowly slide your hands back along the floor until they are parallel with your right knee. Keep the palms face down and the elbows soft.

inhale

- Gently begin to raise your body from the lower back, drawing your shoulders back but keeping the head pointed forward. Do not push with your hands, but use them for support.

exhale

- Continue to raise your body up to sit back on your right foot. Now lift your head fully upright, pushing your shoulders back and chest out. Keep your hips aligned throughout to maintain balance and a correct posture.

inhale

● Recline your head backward and tilt your chin up toward the sky to arch your back. You may need to lift your hands from the floor and support yourself on extended fingertips. Relax and hold the pose for three to six breaths.

● Now lift your body, bearing the weight on your hands and left leg. Bring your right knee out from under your body and lift your hips from the floor. Place the right foot on the floor, then lifting from the toes, bring your tailbone up to straighten your legs.

● Press your chest down toward the floor. Lock your elbows and drop your head between your arms to align with your back, facing toward your toes. Press the soles of your feet and the palms of your hands flat on the floor.

● Straighten your legs and fully extend your arms in an inverted V to take up the Downward Dog *asana* (see pages 38–39). If you wish, you can repeat the sequence on the other side, with your left leg.

exhale II **inhale** ▸ **exhale** **inhale** ▸ **exhale** II

advanced

downward dog into leg raise

prasaritapadasana

Leading on from the Downward Dog, this *asana* strengthens the gluteal, leg, and back muscles, stretches the spine; and loosens the hips. Raise the leg gradually to avoid loosing your balance.

- Do not practice this *asana* if you suffer from back problems. Begin this sequence from the Downward Dog position (see pages 38–39), with the palms of your hands and the soles of your feet resting flat on the floor and your body in an inverted V position.

- Now slowly flex your left knee and raise your left leg from the floor. Straighten the leg as you lift it behind you, maintaining a firm posture with your arms and supporting leg.

- Continue to lift your left leg from the floor and slowly extend it behind you. Reach out with your toes so they are pointed away from the body.

- Now lift your left foot up toward the sky to achieve a full diagonal stretch. Your foot should be pointing at roughly 45 degrees and your leg, back, and arms should form a single straight line. If you find the full extension too difficult, extend only as far as feels comfortable.

inhale ▶ **exhale** ▶ **inhale** ▶

- Hold the pose for three breaths. Remember to keep your hips square throughout to avoid your body twisting out of position.

- To release the pose, exhale while lowering your foot back down toward the floor. Keep your leg straight as you lower it in a single flowing movement.

- Bring your left leg back under your body, relaxing at the knee so you can bring your foot down flat on the floor. Complete the movement to rest in the Downward Dog *asana*.

- Hold for a few breaths before releasing the pose. If you wish, you can repeat the leg raise with the other leg.

exhale II **inhale** ▶ **exhale** ▶ **inhale** ▶ II

advanced

lunging warrior

virasana

This position strengthens the back, legs, hips, shoulders, and arms, and stretches the groin and leg muscles. It also opens the chest and improves both stamina and balance. Be careful with this exercise if you have suffered a knee injury.

- Start the sequence from the Downward Dog *asana* (see pages 38–39), with your feet and hands pressed firmly on the ground and your hips raised in the air so your body forms an inverted V shape.

- Slowly, raise your right leg, lifting from the toes of your left foot. Bring your right leg underneath and into your body so your knee is beneath your chest. Maintain balance with your fingers pressed into the floor and arms locked at the elbows.

inhale

- Now slowly straighten your back and raise your head. Simultaneously, lower your hips toward the floor and stretch your left leg to fully extend. Rest your left knee and the fingertips of both hands on the floor.

exhale

- Slowly raise and outstretch your arms. Bring your hands together, joining at the palms. Tilt your head backward and gradually arch your back. Continue to reach up toward the sky until your face and arms are pointed vertically.

inhale

● Hold the pose for three breaths, breathing deeply. You will feel a stretch in your shoulders and back, and in your groin and thighs.

● Now slowly lower your extended arms, at the same time tilting your head forward. Part your hands and bring your chest down to rest on your right knee with your head facing down toward the floor.

● Press the palms of your hands flat on the floor, in line with your right foot. Now perform the movement in reverse, raising your hips and stepping your feet back to place both soles flat on the floor. Keep your back straight and your arms locked at the elbows.

● Continue to step your feet back until your back is straight and you are again in the inverted V shape of the Downward Dog pose. Repeat the sequence with the other leg.

exhale II **inhale** ▶ **exhale** **inhale** ▶ **exhale** II

standing postures

intermediate

raised mountain

raised tadasana

The Mountain pose (*Tadasana*) is one of the basic yoga *asanas* and forms the foundation for many other poses and sequences. This sequence moves from Downward Dog into a soft forward bend to finish in the Raised Mountain posture. This sequence will strengthen your legs and abdominal muscles, and improve balance and coordination.

- To begin this sequence, take up the Downward Dog position by bringing your tailbone up and pressing your feet and hands flat on the floor so your body forms an inverted V shape (see pages 38–39).

- Now slowly step your feet inward toward your body, one at time. Move them in short steps to avoid putting unnecessary strain on your lower back. Keep your back straight and arms locked at the elbows throughout.

- Keeping the palms of your hands flat on the floor, step your feet into your body until they are between your hands. Now straighten your legs to gain a soft forward bend.

- Hold this pose for three breaths. You will feel a stretch down the back of your thighs and calves. Now wrap your arms around the back of your knees, pressing the inside of your elbow joints into the hollow of your knee joints.

■ inhale ▸ exhale ▸ inhale II exhale

- Keeping your feet firmly on the floor, relax your legs at the knee joints to release the stretch. Clasp your arms together and hug your legs tightly. Hold the pose for a few breaths, breathing deeply into your abdomen.

- Now release the hug and raise your body by slowly straightening your legs. As you straighten your legs, roll your back upward while keeping your head facing the floor. Let your arms hang relaxed at your sides.

- Bring your back upright, but keep the knees soft. Take your hands behind your back and join them together, interlacing your fingers. Pull the shoulders back and extend your arms away from the body. This pose will counterbalance the forward bend.

- Now release the hands and rotate them outward and upward to join at the palms above your head. The movement should be very slow. Straighten your legs at the knees and reach toward the sky as high as you can in the Raised Mountain posture.

inhale **exhale** **inhale** **exhale**

intermediate

intense forward bend

uttanasana

This intense forward bend, or *Uttanasana*, extends and lengthens the body to give the spine a deliberate and intense stretch. This *asana* will stretch the hamstrings, cure stomach pains, and tone the pelvic organs as well as stretch and rejuvenate the spine.

- Do not practice this *asana* if you have recently suffered injuries to your lower back. Begin this sequence from the Raised Mountain posture of the previous exercise (see pages 48–49), keeping your knees tightly together.

- Briefly, raise your body onto your toes, reaching up as high as you can to gain a stretch. Now lower yourself to bring your feet flat on the floor and slowly rotate your arms outward so the palms of your hands are facing down toward the floor.

- As you bring your arms out from the body, bend forward, hinging from the hips. Keep your back straight throughout the movement.

- Continue to bend forward, bringing your head and chest in towards your knees. Keep your legs straight to maintain balance. You will feel an increasing stretch down the backs of your legs as you bend forwards.

inhale ▸ exhale ▸ inhale ▸

● Bring your head into your knees and your hands down to the floor with your palms resting flat. Tuck your head under your body so your forehead touches your shins. Hold the pose for three breaths. You will feel an intense stretch down the back of both legs.

● To come out of the bend, gradually roll your body out straight, first lifting your back. Keep your arms relaxed at the shoulders and hanging at your sides and your chin tucked in.

● Continue to roll your body out from the forward bend by straightening your back and legs before finally bringing your head to face forward. Pull your shoulders back and push your chest forward.

● Standing fully upright, rotate your arms out and bring the palms of your hands together in front of your chest in the *Namaste* pose. Relax and breathe deeply.

exhale ‖ **inhale** ▶ **exhale** **inhale** ▶ **exhale** ■

advanced

wide-legged forward bend

padottanasana "b"

This is an advanced position that stretches the back deeply, relieves stiffness in the legs and hips, and improves elasticity in the hips and spine.

● Do not do practice this *asana* if you have suffered any problems with your hips or lower back. Begin the exercise standing upright with your hands together in *Namaste*.

● Now part your hands and hold them out parallel to your shoulders. Step your feet apart to a distance of three feet, keeping your feet flat on the ground. Bring your arms out from your sides and rotate them down in a circular motion.

● Lower your hands down to your sides to rest on your hips. Slowly bend forward from the hips, keeping your back level and straight.

● As you bend, hold your body weight, on your legs—your neck muscles should not be bearing any weight and your shoulders should be relaxed. You will feel an increasing stretch down the back of your thighs.

exhale ▶ **begin to inhale** ▶ **inhale** ▶

With your feet planted firmly on the floor, continue to bend forward to bring the crown of your head to just above the floor. Keep your hands on your waist and your shoulders and neck relaxed.

Hold the pose for three breaths, breathing deeply and evenly. You will feel an intense stretch down the back of your legs, in your hips, and throughout your lower back.

Now raise your head from the floor, hinging from the hips. Keep your hands on your hips and your back straight throughout the movement.

Once you are standing upright, take your hands away from your hips and extend them out to the sides. Straighten your arms at the elbows to bring them level with your shoulders in the triangle (*Trikonasana*) pose.

exhale ▸ **inhale** II **exhale** **inhale** ▸ **exhale** II

intermediate

extended triangle

trikonasana

The *Trikonasana* (triangle) pose strengthens every part of the body and opens the hips and shoulders. The twist maneuver will also stretch the arms, back, shoulders, and oblique muscles.

- Spread your feet about three feet apart, with toes pointing forward. Extend your arms out from your sides so they are parallel with the floor and level with your shoulders. Keep your palms facing toward the floor.

- Slowly turn your right foot to an angle of 90 degrees so it is pointing in the same direction as your extended right arm.

- Turn your other foot 30 degrees to the right. Keep your feet flat on the floor. Square the hips so they are facing forward, together with your chest and head.

- Hinging from the lower body, slowly reach down to your right. Turning your head to face right, bring your extended right hand down to rest on your shin just below the knee. The movement should cause your left arm to become vertical and point skyward.

inhale ▶ **exhale** ▶ **inhale** ▶

- This pose should create a straight line from your foot to the end of your extended left hand. Look up toward your right hand. Hold the pose for eight breaths. You will feel a stretch in your spine, along the left side of your torso, and across the shoulders.

- To come out of the pose, reverse the movement, hinging from the waist to raise your body upright. Keep your arms straight and level across the shoulders throughout the movement.

- Simultaneously, rotate your right foot back to the starting position to point forward and straighten your left foot.

- Repeat this sequence leaning to the left side. Advanced practitioners can extend the stretch by reaching down to touch the foot.

exhale II **inhale** ▸ **exhale** **inhale** ▸ **exhale** II

standing knee squeeze

Standing knee squeezes, or *Pavanmuktasana*, strengthens the lower back, hips, spine, and legs, and improves balance, posture, and concentration.

- Be careful when practicing this *asana* if you suffer from knee or back problems. Start this exercise in the upright *Tadasana* position (see pages 48–49), with hands together in the prayer position, *Namaste*.

- Slowly raise your right leg, lifting your knee vertically. As you do so, part your hands and extend your arms forward. Your standing leg will need to be slightly soft at the knee for flexible balancing.

- Raise your knee up to waist height and interlock your fingers around the raised knee. Pull the knee toward your body in a gentle hug. While balancing, keep your hips square and avoid twisting your body.

- Hold this pose for three to six breaths. Remember to keep your shoulders down and your spine in a neutral position. You will feel a stretch in your lower back and shoulders.

inhale ▸ **exhale** ▸ **inhale** II **exhale**

● Now lower your leg back to the standing position, bring your hands to your sides, and relax.

● Repeat the raise on the other side, pulling the knee into the body in a gentle hug. Continue to keep your hips square and avoid twisting your body while maintaining balance.

● Hold this pose for three to six breaths, remembering to keep your shoulders down and your spine in a neutral position.

● Now release the leg and return to standing upright. Bring your hands together in *Namaste*. If you wish, you can repeat both lifts two or three times for increased flexibility.

inhale ▸ **inhale** ▸ **inhale** II **exhale** ▸ ■

advanced

forward bend with arm and shoulder stretch

Similar to *Padottanasana "b"* (see pages 52–53), this is an advanced *asana* that deeply stretches the back, legs, and hips, and improves elasticity in the hips and spine. In this variation, the arms and shoulders are also stretched.

- Approach this *asana* with caution if you suffer from lower back or hip problems. Begin the exercise in the intense forward bend pose, with your feet spread three feet apart and the palms of your hands resting flat on the floor.

- Bring your hands up to rest on your hips. Slowly raise your upper body out of the bend, hinging from the hips. Keep your legs and back straight throughout the movement.

- Stand up straight with your back and head upright. Bring your arms out to your sides and then take them behind your back. Clasp your hands together and interlace your fingers.

- Extend your arms behind your back and lock them at the elbows. Pull your shoulders back, push your chest out, and turn your head to face up. You will feel a stretch between the shoulder blades.

exhale ▸ inhale ▸ exhale ▸

- With your feet planted firmly on the floor and locked at the knees, bend forward from the hips to bring your head down toward your legs. Keep your back straight and your arms extended throughout the downward movement.

- Continue the forward bend until your head is facing between your legs. Your interlocked knuckles should be facing away from your body and roughly parallel to the ground. Hold the position for three breaths.

- Keeping your arms fully extended, raise your body upward from the hips, keeping your back straight and spine aligned throughout. Release your clasped hands and let the arms fall to your sides.

- Step your feet in toward the center until they are together. Now bring your hands up to your chest and your palms together in *Namaste*. Face forward, relax, and breath deeply.

inhale ▸ **exhale** **inhale** ▸ **exhale** ■

side-angle posture

parsvakonasana

This sequence moves through the Warrior pose and into the Side-angle Posture, toning up the ankles, knees, and thighs. It corrects defects in the calves and thighs, expands the chest, and helps to reduce fat around the waist and hips.

- Approach this *asana* with caution if you suffer from neck problems. Begin standing in *Tadasana* (see pages 48–49) with your hands together in the prayer pose, *Namaste*.

- Slowly open out your body to take up the *Trikonasana* pose. Part the hands and take them out to the sides.

- Spread your feet about three feet apart, with toes pointing forward. Extend your arms out from your sides so they are parallel to the floor, and hold them level with your shoulders. Keep your palms facing down toward the floor.

- From the triangle position, rotate your right foot so that it is 90 degrees to the body and pointing in the same direction as your right arm.

inhale ▸ exhale ▸ inhale ▸

● Now bend your right leg at the knee until the thigh and calf form a right angle and the right thigh is parallel to the floor. Hold the Warrior pose for six breaths. You will feel pressure on your right knee and a stretch in your left thigh.

● Now lean your upper body to the right and bring your right elbow down to rest on your extended knee. Turn your head to the left to face up at a 45-degree angle.

● Pull your left shoulder back and extend your left arm behind your back to rest the hand on the inside of your right thigh. Hold this pose for three to six breaths. You will feel a stretch down the left side of your body.

● Now release the stretch and return to the start position, bringing your body upright, spreading your legs wide, and extending your arms out from the shoulders. For counter-balance, repeat on the other leg.

exhale ▶ **inhale** **exhale** II **exhale** ▶ II

padottanasana "a" into lunging twist

This sequence is based on *Parivrtta Parsvakonasana*, but as a lunge. It will help build up lower body strength and improve blood circulation around the abdominal organs and the spinal column. The sequence continues on the following pages.

- Take up *Trikonasana* by spreading your feet about three feet apart. Extend your arms out from your sides so they are parallel to the floor and level with your shoulders. Keep your palms facing down toward the floor.

- Bring your arms into your waist and rest your hands on your hips with elbows extended out to the sides. Hinging from the waist, slowly bend your upper body forward.

- Continue to bend forward, bringing your head down toward the floor. Keep your back straight throughout the bend. Your thigh muscles will tense as they take the strain of the forward movement.

- As your head reaches waist height, bring your hands away from your hips and place your extended fingers on the floor. Support the body weight by resting your palms flat, then continue the forward bend until your head is almost touching the floor.

inhale ▶ **exhale** ▶ **inhale** ▶

● Hold this pose for three to six breaths, breathing deeply. You will feel a stretch down the backs of your thighs and in your lower back.

● Now raise your body slightly and walk your hands around your extended right leg until your head is opposite your knee. Moving onto your toes, turn your feet to point to the right at the same time.

● Now bend your right knee and bring your chest down onto the knee, while simultaneously extending your left leg backward so your knee and shin rest flat on the floor. Rotate your trunk to the right and bring the left arm over your right knee.

● Rest your left armpit on the outer side of the right knee and bring both hands together to clench beside your right hip. Your head should be facing roughly 90 degrees to your body. Hold the pose for six breaths.

exhale II **inhale** ▶ **exhale** **inhale** ▶ **exhale** II

advanced

lunging twist (continued)

parivrtta parsvakonasana

This sequence is a continuation of the previous pages, and offers a counterbalancing deep forward bend to the lunging twist. Not suitable for beginners, it helps to develop flexibility in the spine.

- Continue the move from the twisted side bend on the previous page. Slowly, bring your body out of the twist by lifting your left hand back over your knee.

- Straighten your trunk, then lean your head forward and bring both hands down to rest the palms flat on the floor. Balanced on your toes, raise your hips, with your left leg extended backward and your right leg forward and bent at the knee.

inhale

- While maintaining a forward bend, raise your body slightly and walk your hands to the left, rotating your body from the hips back to the center line. Keep your back straight throughout this movement.

exhale

- Again, place your palms flat on the floor to take your body weight. Lower the crown of your head close to the floor so you are looking back between your extended legs. Your legs should be locked at the knees.

inhale

- Hold this pose for three to six breaths, breathing deeply. You will feel a stretch down the back of your thighs and in your lower back.

- Now release the bend and slowly raise your body, remembering to keep your back straight. Your thigh muscles will tense as they take the strain of the body being raised from the waist.

- Bring your arms into your waist and rest your hands on your hips with elbows extended out to the sides. Continue to raise your upper body until your are standing upright, with feet spread wide apart.

- Now step your legs back into the center, and stand upright in *Tadasana*. Bring your hands together in the prayer pose, *Namaste*, and rest.

exhale II **inhale** ▸ **exhale** **inhale** ▸ **exhale** ■

intermediate

tree *vrksasana*

This *asana* tones the leg muscles, opens the hips, and improves balance, coordination, and concentration. Approach this sequence cautiously if you have weak knees or ankles.

- Begin from the standing pose, *Tadasana*, with your hands together in *Namaste*. If you think you will have problems balancing in this sequence, stand near a wall for support.

- Part your hands and bring them down in front of your body. As you do so, bend your left leg and raise it up to waist height. Bring your left hand down to meet your rising left knee.

inhale

- Now grip your left ankle with your left hand and lift the sole of the foot toward the right leg to rest at the top of the inside of the thigh. If you find this too difficult, place the sole of your foot just above the knee, or as near to the top of the thigh as you can manage.

exhale

- Hold the position, maintaining balance on your standing leg. Bring your hands together in the *Namaste mudra*. Now gently raise your arms above your head, extending them as far as you can while keeping the palms pressed together.

inhale

● Hold this pose for three to six breaths, breathing deeply. Keep your stomach muscles relaxed throughout. You will feel a stretch in your hips, thighs, the knee of the raised leg, and in the ankles.

● Keeping your feet steady, extend your arms out and bring them down to your sides in a smooth, circular motion. Try to keep your trunk steady throughout this movement. You might want to fix your eyes on a point in front of you to aid balance.

● Continue the downward movement of the hands, then bring them around in a circle and up in front of your chest, where you can join the palms together. Simultaneously, lower your left leg to the floor, keeping steady on your standing leg.

● Return to the upright *Tadasana* position, with your hands joined in *Namaste*. Repeat the exercise with the other leg.

exhale ‖ **inhale** ▶ **exhale** **inhale** ▶ **exhale** ■

intermediate

dancer *natarajasana*

This sequence strengthens your legs, feet, and lower back, and opens the hips and pelvis. The forward stretch and counterposed standing knee squeeze require a great deal of balance and should only be attempted by advanced practitioners.

● Approach this exercise with caution if you suffer from back or foot problems. Begin the exercise in *Tadasana*, standing upright with your hands together in *Namaste*.

● Raise your right knee, then flex your leg to bring your foot up toward your buttocks. Bring your arms down to your sides; then move your right hand toward your right foot. Grip your right ankle with your right hand and hold this position.

● Raise your left hand and extend the arm skyward, while maintaining balance on your left foot. Keep the toes of your standing leg flat on the floor. To aid balance, you could fix your eyes on a point in front of you. Keep your head up and facing forward.

● Now slowly lean your chest forward and extend your right leg, using your right arm for leverage. Flexing the knee, extend your right leg back until your right arm is fully stretched. Point your left arm at 45 degrees. Make sure you are holding the front of the foot.

inhale ▶ begin to exhale ▶ exhale ▶

● Hold this pose for three breaths. Relax your stomach muscles and breath normally. You will feel a stretch in the thigh of your lifted leg. Now release the stretch and bring your right knee forward and back under your body, while slowly lowering your left arm.

● To begin the counterpose, bring your knee up toward your chest. At the same time, bring your left arm down and interlace the fingers of both hands around the raised knee.

● Pulling inward with both hands, gently press the thigh of your raised knee against your chest. You will need to tilt your hips upward to maintain an upright posture. Hold the pose for three breaths.

● Now release the knee and lower the foot back down to the floor. Return to the upright standing pose with hands in *Namaste*. Now repeat the sequence with your left leg.

exhale II **inhale** ▸ **exhale** **inhale** ▸ **exhale** ■

sitting postures

intermediate

seated staff *dandasana*

This sequence begins with a deep forward bend before moving into *Dandasana*, the Seated Staff. The movement will tone the abdomen and relieve bloatedness and gas in the stomach, as well as extend and lengthen the body to give the spine an intense stretch.

- Begin this exercise standing upright in *Tadasana*, with your hands together in *Namaste*. You are going to begin with an intense forward bend, *Uttanasana* (see pages 50–51).

- Hinging from the hips, bend your chest down toward your knees. Simultaneously bring your hands down toward the floor. Keep your back straight throughout the movement.

- If it is uncomfortable to keep your legs straight as you bend forward, then bend them slightly. Tuck your head under your body, so your forehead is facing your shins. Press your chest toward your knees.

- Position your hands so your forearms are parallel with your legs and the palms of your hands are pressing flat on the floor. Hold the bend for three breaths.

II inhale ▸ exhale ▸ inhale II exhale

● Now bend at the knees and lower your hips toward the floor. Keep your hands on the floor throughout this downward movement, balancing on your fingertips.

● As your tailbone nears the floor, take your left leg forward and extend your foot to rest your heel on the floor. Use your hands to help maintain balance. Tilt your head forward to center your body weight.

● Continue to move into a seated position, simultaneously extending your right leg forward. Put the palms of your hands flat on the floor and take the weight as you bring your legs into an outstretched seated position.

● Relax in the upright seated position, with your back straight, your palms flat on the floor at your sides, and your chest pushed forward.

inhale ▶ exhale

inhale ▶ exhale ■

advanced

seated forward bend

paschimottanasana

This *asana* will stretch and lengthen the spine and hamstrings, open the back, and tone and massage the abdominal organs while improving digestion.

● Approach this *asana* with caution if you suffer from lower back problems. Begin this exercise in the seated, upright posture, with your palms flat on the floor and your legs extended but slightly soft at the knees. Your toes should be pointing up.

● Raise your hands and reach them above your head, bringing them in line with each other (but not touching). Raise your knees three inches off the ground and point your toes forward. Keep your back straight and hips aligned.

● Hinging from the hips, bend forward. It is important that you bend from the pelvis, and not the middle back, to obtain the correct posture and achieve a full stretch of the spine.

● Continue to bend forward until your forehead touches your shins. Wrap your arms under your knees and hold the pose for six breaths. You will feel a stretch along the length of your spine and in your hamstrings.

■ exhale ▶ inhale ▶ exhale II inhale

- Now release the stretch and raise your head, bringing your back up to a 45-degree angle. Place your hands on your thighs, then slide them forward along the length of your legs toward your feet.

- Rest your head on your shins and hold the soles of your feet with the fingers of both hands. Gently pull the soles to bring your legs straight and extend the stretch. If you can, move your hands to hold the soles of your feet to gain a more intense stretch.

- Hold the pose for three breaths. You will feel an intense stretch in the lower back, along the length of the spine, and in the hamstring muscles.

- Release the stretch. Slide your hands back toward your body and keep your back straight as you return to an upright seated position. Rest your palms flat on the floor and relax.

exhale ▶ **inhale** ▶ **exhale** II **inhale** ▶ **exhale** II

back arch

purvottanasana

This *asana* is an introduction to *Purvottanasana*. It stretches and tones the abdomen and chest. It will strengthen the wrists, improve shoulder flexibility, and expand the chest. It is also a good counterbalance to forward bending *asanas*, such as the Seated Forward Bend (see pages 74–75).

- Approach this *asana* with caution if you suffer from lower back problems. Begin this exercise in the seated, upright posture, with your palms flat on the floor and your legs extended but slightly soft at the knees. Your toes should be pointing up.

- Slowly extend your arms behind your back, walking your fingers along the floor until they are roughly 15 inches away from your body. Keep your chest pushed forward throughout this movement.

- Rest your palms flat on the floor with your fingers pointing forward, toward your body. Now slowly lean your head back, keeping your arms locked at the elbows.

- Extend your head back until the chin is pointing at the sky. Arch your back to stretch your abdomen and expand your chest. Keep your shoulders level and try not to hunch throughout the movement.

inhale ▸ begin to exhale ▸ exhale ▸

- Tilt your head back as far as it will go without causing pain, and push your chest out. Hold the pose for three to six breaths, breathing deeply. You will feel a stretch in your abdomen and chest.

- Slowly release the pose and bring your body back to an upright position. Lift your hands and bring them in toward your body.

- Bring your hands alongside your buttocks and relax your shoulders. Complete the move by returning to the start position, sitting upright, with your legs extended and palms resting flat on the floor at your sides.

- If you wish, you can repeat this movement a number of times to stretch your abdominal muscles and improve spinal flexibility.

inhale II **exhale** **inhale** ▸ **exhale** ▸ ■

head to knee (1)

janusirsasana

This gentle stretch will prepare you for the full posture on the following pages. It is a good foundation *asana* for the beginner wishing to develop better spinal flexibility.

- Begin the preparatory stretch in the seated upright posture, with your palms flat on the floor. Your legs should be fully extended but slightly soft at the knees, with the toes pointing up.

- Move your left leg out to the side, at about 20 degrees from your center line. Bend the right leg and bring it into the body so the heel and sole of the foot rest against the inside of your left thigh. Use your right hand to help ease it into position.

- Once your right knee is in position, return your hand to your side. Raise your head and push your shoulders back. Keep your back straight.

- Now gently rotate your upper body to the right. Rotate from the waist, keeping your hips aligned, and try not to put any body weight on the right hand.

■ ‖ inhale ▸ exhale ▸ inhale ▸

● Continue the rotation and bring your eft hand over to rest on your right knee. Simultaneously pull your right shoulder back and turn your head to face right.

● Extend the stretch as far as you can without feeling discomfort. Hold the pose for six breaths, keeping your chest pushed out, your shoulders back, and your hips aligned.

● Release the stretch and gently bring your head and body back to the left to face forward, rotating from the waist. Keep your hand rested on your right knee and your back straight.

● Counterbalance the stretch by repeating the movement in the other direction, tucking in your left leg and rotating to the left.

exhale **inhale** II **exhale** **inhale** ▶ **exhale** II

advanced

head to knee (2)

janusirsasana

The second part of the movement extends the spine and is for advanced practitioners only. This movement will stimulate the kidneys, liver, and pancreas; stretch and strengthen the leg muscles; and stimulate blood circulation to the spine.

- Beginning from the twisted seated position of the previous exercise (see page 79), rotate your upper body from the waist to face in the direction of your extended left leg.

- Looking down toward your extended toes, reach out with your right hand and bend your body forward, hinging from the waist. Exhale as you bend forward.

- Move your left arm forward to continue the forward bend until you can hold the sole of the left foot with both hands. Keep the elbows soft throughout the reach.

- Fully extend your upper body and lower your head down to rest on your left shin. You will feel an intense stretch in your left hamstring muscles, your lower back, and along the length of your spine.

inhale exhale ▸ inhale ▸ exhale ▸

● Hold the pose for three to six breaths, or for as long as it feels comfortable.

● Now release the foot, inhale, and raise your body up and away from the extended leg. Lift from the waist, straightening your back as you do so.

● Once your body is upright, bring your right hand down to your right ankle and lead the leg away from the inside of the opposite thigh. Slowly extend your right leg to rest on the floor, and bring both feet together.

● Straighten your back and place your arms by your sides with palms facing flat on the floor. Now repeat the *asana* with the right leg extended.

inhale ‖ **exhale** **inhale** ▶ **exhale** ▶ ■

seated spinal twist

marichyasana

The Seated Spinal Twist, or *Marichyasana*, will help strengthen the back and relieve backache, lumbago, and pains in the hips. It will also strengthen the neck muscles and make the shoulders more flexible.

- Begin this sequence in the seated, upright posture, *Dandasana* (see pages 72–73). Your legs should be extended but slightly soft at the knees and together at the ankles, with your hands resting palms down at your sides.

- Now slowly raise your right knee, placing the sole of the foot flat on the floor so it rests besides the left knee joint. Bring your left hand across and pull the knee into the body. Keep your left leg extended and flat on the floor.

- Wrap your left arm around your raised right knee and twist your body to the right. Rotate from the waist, keeping your hips square and aligned.

- Keep your shoulders aligned and bring your right hand back to rest flat on the floor to your right, in line with your buttocks, with fingers pointing away from the body. This will help you extend the twist and provide stability and balance for the pose.

inhale ▸ exhale ▸ inhale ▸

● To achieve the full spinal twist, turn your head to look along your right shoulder, in the opposite direction to your extended left leg. You will feel a stretch in your neck.

● Hold the pose for six breaths. You will feel a stretch along the length of your spine, in the oblique muscles at the sides of your torso, and in the gluteal muscles of your right buttock.

● Now rotate your upper body back to the left, bringing your right hand off the floor. Release the knee as you return to face in the same direction as your extended leg. Keep your back straight throughout the movement.

● Rest your right leg flat on the floor. Return to *Dandasana*, sitting upright with a straight back and with the palms of your hands resting flat on the floor at your sides.

exhale **inhale** **II** **exhale** **inhale** ▶ **exhale** ■

intermediate

bound angle posture (supine)

The supine *Baddhakonasana*, or Bound Angle Posture, will lengthen the abdomen and open the chest, and stretch the adductor muscles on the insides of the thighs.

- Begin this exercise seated. Bend your knees and bring the soles and heels of your feet together, holding your ankles with your hands. The outside of your feet should rest flat against the floor. Your head should be tilted down.

- Gripping your feet firmly, sit up to stretch the spine erect. Raise your head and gaze straight in front or at the tip of your nose.

- Now bring your hands away from your feet and move them behind your back, while at the same time tilting your body forward.

- Place your hands flat on the floor just behind your back, with the fingers pointed forward (this will keep your shoulders aligned). Extend your arms fully to lock at the elbow.

inhale ▸ exhale ▸ inhale ▸

● Slowly, begin to lean backward, taking your body weight as you lower your back toward the ground. Keep facing forward throughout the movement, and move your arms out to the sides to support your body.

● Lower your back slowly, vertebrae by vertebrae, until it is flat on the floor. Throughout the movement, keep the heels and soles of your feet pressed firmly together.

● Now raise your arms to bring your hands together and interlock the fingers. Put your interlocked hands behind your head to give support. Lower your head back to rest flat on the floor.

● Keep your knees pushed out wide, and as close to the ground as you can, while making sure that the soles of your feet remain pressed together. Hold this pose for six breaths. You will feel a stretch in the adductor muscles along the inside of your thighs.

begin to exhale **exhale** ▶ **inhale** ▶ **exhale** ❚❚

intermediate

bound angle posture (forward bend)

Following on from the supine Bound Angle Posture of the previous page, this sequence will stimulate the abdomen, pelvis, and back by increasing the blood supply. It can also relieve urinary disorders.

- Begin this exercise in the finished position of the previous one, lying on the ground, with the soles of your feet pressed together and your hands interlocked and behind your head.

- Slowly take your hands out from under your head and bring them over and forward toward the floor. Rest the elbows and forearms flat on the floor at your sides.

- Simultaneously, begin to raise your upper body from the floor, lifting from the abdomen. If you need to, use your elbows to help push yourself off the floor. Remember to keep the soles and heels of your feet together throughout the movement.

- Raise your body into the upright position, then continue the movement by bending forward. Hinge from the waist and keep your knees pressed on the floor throughout.

exhale ▶ **inhale** ▶ **exhale** ▶

- As you bend, bring your hands to the front and grip your feet at the ankles. Continue to bend forward, bringing your head down toward the floor and arching your back.

- Place your elbows on your extended thighs and press down. Exhale, then bend forward to bring your head close to your feet. Hold the pose for three to six breaths, or for as long as it feels comfortable without causing a strain.

- Inhale and raise your trunk from the floor, rolling your body out in a smooth, graceful movement. Keep the soles of your feet pressed together and your hands gently pressed down on your ankles throughout the movement.

- Bring your head upright, straighten your back, and face forward. Relax and breathe deeply.

inhale ▸ **exhale** II **inhale** ▸ **exhale** II

intermediate

extended angle pose

upavisthakonasana

This *asana* starts from *Baddhakonasana* and moves into a wide-legged stretch. The sequence will stretch your groin and lower back, and improve circulation in your legs.

● Begin this exercise in the final position of the Bound Angle Posture (see pages 86–87), sitting upright with your back straight and the heels of the soles of your feet pressed flat together.

● Now remove your hands from your ankles and slowly bring your feet apart, extending your legs out from the center. Keep your back upright, your shoulders back, and hips square throughout this movement.

● Spread your legs out wide so they form a 90-degree angle. Extend your legs until they are flat on the floor and locked at the knees. Flex your feet with toes pointing up. You will feel a stretch along the inside of your thighs.

● Now begin to bend forward. Put your hands in front of you for support, pushing them away from the body as you continue the forward bend.

inhale ▶ exhale ▶ inhale ▶

- Gently continue to reach forward until your arms are fully extended. Face down toward the floor with your toes pointed vertically.

- Hold the pose for three breaths, taking care not to overextend and damage your lower back or hips. You will feel a stretch along the backs and inside of your thighs, around your pelvis, and in your lower back.

- Now raise yourself out of the stretch by lifting your back and sliding your hands back toward your body. Lift from the torso, using your arms to help maintain balance.

- Return to sit fully upright, with your legs extended but relaxed. Keep your back straight, bring your shoulders back, and rest your hands on your thighs. Relax and breathe deeply.

exhale ▶ **inhale** II **exhale** **inhale** ▶ **exhale** II

intermediate

sacred cow (1)

gomukhasana

This *asana* will improve posture by loosening up the shoulder joints and strengthening the muscles in the upper back and arms. It is a particularly good exercise for people who use computers daily.

- Approach this *asana* with caution if you suffer from neck or back problems. Begin the sequence sitting on the floor with your knees tucked in toward your body. Hug your knees with your arms and tilt your body back to balance on your buttocks.

inhale

- Use your hands to guide your right knee over your left knee. Now tuck your left leg under the hollow of your right knee so your legs are crossed and both knees are pointing forward from the center of the body.

exhale

- Place the palms of your hands flat on the floor at your sides and adjust your position so that your hips are square, your shoulders are level, and your back is straight and upright.

inhale

- Bring your hands into the center of the body to rest on the knees. Now raise your right arm and start to reach over your head behind your back, between your shoulder blades, with your palm facing in toward the body.

exhale

● Simultaneously, take your left arm down and bend it behind your back into a vertical position with your palm facing out along the center of the spine.

● Now join your hands by hooking your fingers and interlocking them together. (If you have difficulty joining your hands together, hold a small towel to obtain a stretch.) Maintain a neutral spine and remember not to arch your back.

● Hold this pose for six breaths, remembering to keep your back straight and upright. You will feel a stretch between your shoulder blades and in the shoulders and arms.

● Come out of the position by unlinking your hands and lifting your feet. Now turn to the next page to practice the *asana* with your arms reversed.

inhale ▶ **exhale** **text** ▶ **inhale** II **exhale** II

intermediate

sacred cow (2)

gomukhasana

This sequence continues from the previous pages, practicing the Sacred Cow on the opposite side. If you can't link the hands together fully, try using just the fingers in an S grip. Make sure the elbow is pushed back as far as it can go.

- Begin this sequence with your hands linked in the final stretch of the previous page. Slowly unlink your hands and bring them back in front of your body.

- Now uncross your legs, guiding your left leg out from under your right leg with your hands. Bring both knees together and hug them into your body, holding the pose briefly to gain a counterstretch along the spine.

- Now release your legs and use your hands to guide your left knee over your right knee. Tuck your right leg under the hollow of your left knee so your legs are crossed and both knees are pointing forward from the center of the body.

- Adjust your position so your hips are square, your shoulders are level, and your back is straight and upright. Rest your hands on your knees.

inhale ▸ exhale ▸ inhale ▸

- Now raise your left arm up and reach over your head, between your shoulder blades, with your palm facing in. Simultaneously, twist your right arm under and behind your back into a vertical position with your palm facing out along the center of the spine.

- Now join your hands by hooking your fingers and interlocking them together. (If you have difficulty joining your hands, hold a small towel to achieve the stretch.) Maintain a neutral spine and remember not to arch your back.

- Hold this pose for six breaths, remembering to keep your back upright. You will feel a stretch between your shoulder blades and in the shoulders and arms. Unlink your hands and bring them forward to rest on your knees.

- Use your hands to take your feet out of the cross-legged position. Bring your knees up and in line and hug them together toward your chest in a counterpose. Hold briefly before releasing the pose and relaxing.

begin to exhale ▶ **exhale** **inhale** II **exhale** ▶ II

seated full spinal twist (1)

ardha matsyendrasana

This *asana* realigns the vertebrae, adding strength and flexibility to the spine, and massages the internal organs, improving liver and kidney functions and digestion. The twisting movement also strengthens the arms, shoulders, and neck muscles.

- Begin this sequence in the finishing pose of the previous *asana*, tilted back on your buttocks with your arms wrapped around your knees and hugging your knees into your chest.

- Now release the hug and lower your left leg to the floor. Bring your right leg up and over your left leg, so the left is resting with the side of the thigh flat on the floor and tucked beneath the right leg.

- Bring your right leg over your left knee and rest the sole of the foot flat on the floor and pressed against the outside of the bended knee. Wrap your left arm around your raised left knee and hug your knee toward your body. Inhale and lift the spine out of the pelvis.

- Rotating from the waist, twist your body to the right, keeping your hips square. Bring your right hand back to rest flat on the floor to your right side, in line with your buttocks. This will help you extend the twisted pose.

exhale ▸ inhale ▸ exhale ▸

● Face your head right and look along your right shoulder, at 90 degrees to your hips. Hold the pose for six breaths. You will feel a stretch along the length of your spine and in the gluteal muscles of your right buttock.

● Now release the stretch and rotate your body to face forward, bringing both hands to rest on your raised knee. Keep your back straight.

● Lift your left foot over the other knee, then tilt your body backward and bring the right leg out from under the other leg. Realign your legs by bringing them together at the ankles and knees.

● Now bring both legs back together, resting the soles of your feet flat on the floor in preparation for practicing the spinal twist in the opposite direction (see pages 96–97).

inhale II **exhale** ▶ **inhale** **exhale** ▶ II

seated full spinal twist (2)

ardha matsyendrasana

This sequence continues the spinal twist from the previous page, twisting the body to the left. It is important to perform the twist in both directions to realign the vertebrae and rebalance the spinal fluid.

- Begin this sequence as you finished the previous *asana*, with feet flat on the ground and your knees drawn up to your chest.

- Now bring your left leg up and over your right leg, so the right is resting with the side of the thigh flat on the floor and tucked beneath the raised left knee.

- Bring your left leg over your right knee and rest the sole of the foot flat on the floor and pressed against the side of your bended knee. Wrap your right arm around your raised right knee and hug your knee toward your body. Inhale and lift the spine out of the pelvis.

- Twist your body to the left, rotating from the waist. Keep your hips square and aligned. Bring your left hand back to rest flat on the floor to your left, in line with your buttocks. This will help you extend and hold the twisted pose.

inhale ▸ exhale ▸ inhale ▸

● Keep your shoulders square and aligned. Face your head in the same direction as your chest, at 90 degrees to your hips.

● Hold the pose for six breaths. You will feel a stretch along the length of your spine and in the gluteal muscles of your left buttock.

● Now release the stretch and rotate your body back to face forward. Lift your left foot over the other knee, then tilt yourself backward and bring the right leg out from underneath your body.

● Return to sitting upright in the Thunderbolt pose, with your feet tucked under your buttocks, your spine straight, and your hands resting at your sides.

exhale inhale II exhale inhale ▶ exhale II

intermediate

supta vajrasana

thunderbolt into kneeling back bend

This sequence moves from the seated upright Thunderbolt pose to a full kneeling back bend. The two-part movement will mobilize your back muscles, hips, and ankles; improve spinal flexibility; relieve lower back tension; and help flatten your stomach.

- Sit back on your haunches with your feet tucked under your buttocks in the Thunderbolt pose. Keep your back straight, head upright, and arms relaxed by your sides.

- Hinging from the waist, gently recline your back toward the floor. Simultaneously move your arms behind to provide support, first balancing on your fingertips.

- Walk your fingers back and away from the body until they are roughly eight inches away from your extended toes. This will help you achieve a more pronounced back bend.

- Lower your back until your palms are resting flat on the floor with your fingertips facing into the body. Once your body weight is fully supported by your arms, push your chest out and gently roll your head back to face the sky. Hold the pose for three breaths.

inhale ▶ **exhale** ▶ **inhale** II **exhale**

- To enter the second part of the sequence, bend your elbows and continue to lower your body. You will feel some strain in your abdominal muscles, which bear the weight as you continue the movement.

- Bring your arms underneath your back so the palms of your hands are touching the soles of your feet and your elbows and forearms are resting flat on the floor.

- Resting on your elbows, throw your head backward and point your chin toward the sky. Expand your chest up. You will feel a stretch in your stomach and chest.

- Continue to thrust your chest up while reclining your head back as far as it will go without causing discomfort. Hold the pose for three breaths. Now relax and return to the upright seated position.

inhale ▶ **exhale** ▶ **inhale** ▶ **exhale** II

extended child

balasana

This is a gradual movement that achieves a full stretch while in the relaxed Child *asana*. The basic Child pose relaxes the lower back and neck while improving circulation and reducing fatigue and tension. By extending the arms, you can also stretch the shoulders and upper back muscles.

- Begin this sequence sitting upright in the Thunderbolt *asana* (see page 98) with your legs tucked under your body, your buttocks gently resting back on your heels, and your hands at your sides with your fingers extended to touch the floor.
- Hinging from the waist, slowly lower your chest forward, maintaining a straight back throughout the forward movement.
- Continue to bend forward until your chest is pressed into your thighs and your forehead is resting flat on the floor. Let gravity pull your arms to the ground and rest the tops of your hands flat on the floor.
- Relax your neck, shoulders, and arms and breathe deeply. Hold the pose for three to six breaths.

■ inhale ▸ exhale ▸ inhale II exhale

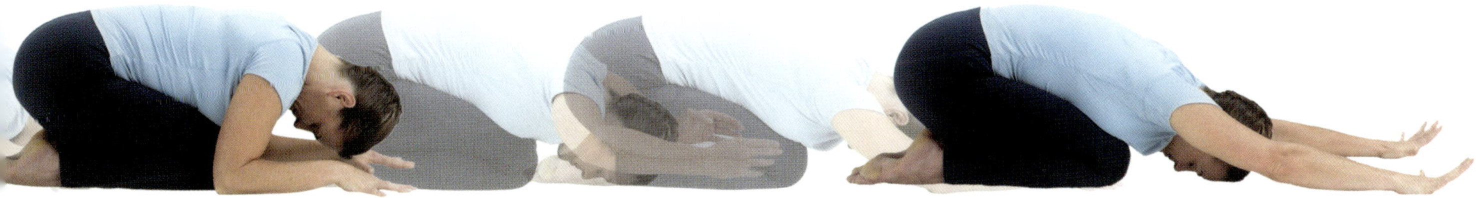

Keeping your forehead pressed on the floor, lift your elbows and walk your hands forward and past your head, keeping your hands in line throughout the movement.

Continue to extend your arms forward until you are reaching as far as you can without lifting your body from the floor.

Extend your arms fully to reach out with your fingers pointed forward. Hold the pose for six breaths, breathing deeply into the abdomen. You will feel a stretch along your shoulders and in the muscles of your upper back.

To come out of the position, slowly raise your head and roll your body upward while using your hands to support your body. Return to the start position, sitting upright and facing forward in the Thunderbolt *asana*.

inhale ▸ **exhale** II ▸ II

finishing postures

intermediate

sethubandhasana

supine curl from extended child

This movement begins in Extended Child and moves through a supine curl and returns to the semi-supine start position for the Pelvic Lift (see pages 106–107).

- Begin this movement in the Child *asana* (see pages 100–101), crouching with your knees drawn under your body, your toes pointed out, and the palms of your hands and forehead aligned and pressed flat on the floor.
- Draw your arms in toward your body and gently roll over to your right so you are lying on your right side and facing left.
- Continue the roll until your shoulders are resting flat on the floor, followed by your back. Keep your knees bent and tucked in toward the body throughout the movement.
- Bring your knees into your chest and gently pull the thighs into the abdomen to release the lower back and lift your buttocks from the floor. Grip your knees with your hands and hug your knees in toward your chest.

■ II **inhale** ▸ **exhale** ▸ **inhale** ▸

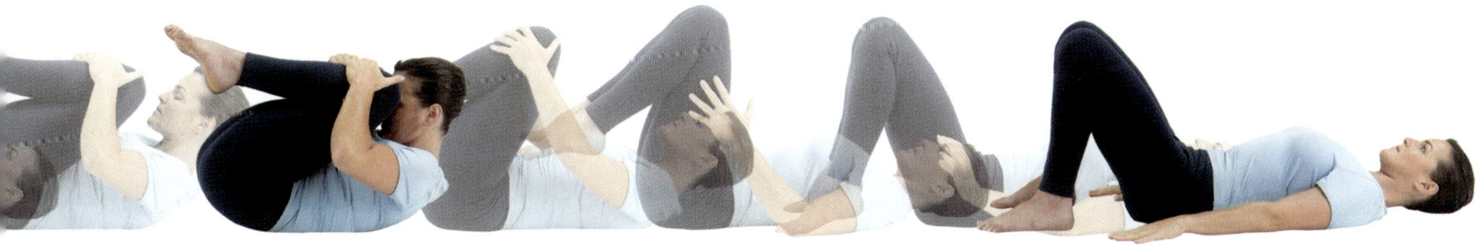

● Lift your head to touch your forehead against your knees with your toes pointed and parallel to the floor. This position will cause your back to arch out and counterbalance the pelvic lift on the next page.

● Hold the pose for three to six breaths. You will feel a stretch along your spine and in the neck. Release your knees and lower your legs back down to the floor, resting the soles of your feet flat.

● Simultaneously, lower your head and shoulders to rest flat on the floor. Bring your arms back down to your sides, with the palms facing down and flat on the floor.

● Complete the movement with your back and buttocks flat on the floor and your hands resting at your sides. Relax and breathe deeply.

exhale **inhale** II **exhale** **inhale** ▶ **exhale** ■

intermediate

pelvic lift

setubandhasana

This movement will strengthen your neck and back muscles, mobilize your neck and shoulders, and improve spinal flexibility. It will also firm your legs, thighs, hips, and bottom.

- Begin this movement lying on your back with your knees bent, your feet flat on the floor, and your arms resting at your sides. Now draw your knees in toward your chest and bring your hands up to grip your knees.

- Pulling with your hands, gently hug your knees into your chest, keeping your shoulders and head flat on the floor. This will help mobilize your spine in preparation for the pelvic lift.

- Hold the pose briefly before releasing the stretch. Lower your legs back down and plant your feet on the floor, roughly hip-width apart and close to the buttocks in preparation for the pelvic lift. Bring your arms to rest flat on the floor, palms facing down.

- Inhale and lift your hips from the floor. Slowly raise your back in a smooth, rolling movement that starts from your upper back and shoulders and extends down to your buttocks. As you lift, keep your buttocks squeezed together for stability.

inhale **exhale** ▶ ▶ **inhale** ▶

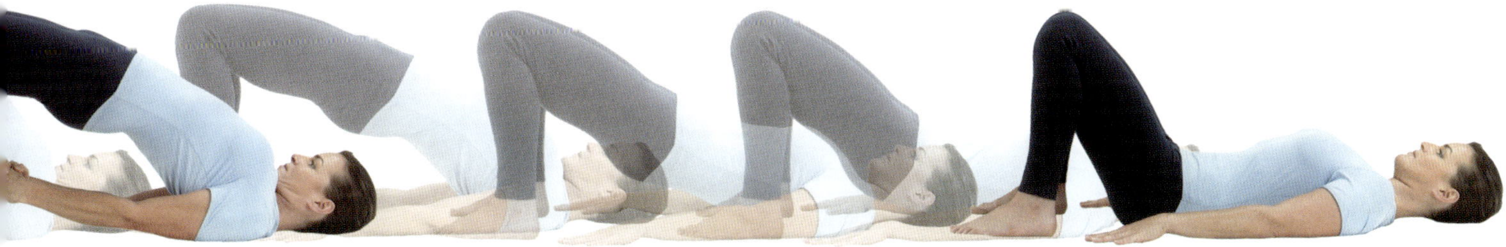

Keep your arms and hands pressed into the floor. You will feel your chin push into your chest as the back of your neck lengthens. Hold this pose for three to six breaths, or for as long as it feels comfortable.

While maintaining the pelvic lift, bring your hands under your body and together. Interlace your fingers and straighten your arms to lock at the elbow. This will bring your shoulders away from the floor, opening your shoulders and strengthening the arms.

Hold this pose for three breaths. Release your hands and rest them flat on the floor. Now gently lower your pelvis down toward the floor. Remember to keep your buttocks flexed to provide stability and support.

Complete the movement resting with your back flat on the floor, your knees raised, and your hands resting at your sides. Relax and breathe deeply.

exhale II **inhale** ▸ **exhale** **inhale** II ▸ **exhale** ■

advanced

shoulder stand *salamba sarvanghasana*

This is an advanced position that strengthens your entire body and directs circulation toward your thyroid gland. It requires a great deal of body strength and balance. For safety, always practice on a padded but firm support to protect the neck.

- For this movement, you might want to use a pillow or towel to protect your shoulders. Begin the exercise lying on your back, facing the sky with your knees bent and the soles of your feet flat on the floor.

- Lay your arms on the floor, parallel to your body with your palms facing down. Slowly pull your knees up together, keeping them aligned throughout the raise.

- Continue to raise your knees, lifting your feet to point vertically. Then bring your knees in toward your chest. Keep your legs bent at the knees throughout the movement.

- Bring your knees fully into your chest. Your center of gravity will begin to shift, lifting your lower back from the floor. Pressing down with your palms and forearms, raise your hips vertically from the floor.

inhale ▸ **begin to exhale** ▸ **exhale** ▸

- Now lift your hips, gradually rolling your back off the floor and lifting your legs. As you push your hips up, bring your hands up to support your lower back, with your fingers pointing in toward the spine.

- Lift your legs, keeping your toes pointed. Maintain your center of gravity. The lifting movement should come from the shoulders. Keep your hands on your lower back to provide support throughout the lift.

- Straighten out your legs from the knees and raise your lower back to a 90-degree angle. Feel your body lift from the base of your neck. For a full shoulder stand, your back and legs should form a vertical line.

- Press your chin into your neck. Hold the pose for six breaths, or for as long as it feels comfortable.

inhale ▸ **exhale** **inhale** ▸ **exhale** ‖

advanced

plow *halasana*

The plow pose strengthens the hamstrings, abdomen, ankles, and feet. It relieves stiffness in the shoulders and neck, and increases spinal flexibility. This sequence follows on directly from the Shoulder Stand (see pages 108–109), and can only be attempted by those who have mastered this earlier *asana*.

- Do not attempt this exercise if you have suffered an injury to your neck or spine. Begin this *asana* in the shoulder stand pose (see pages 110–111), with your legs extended upright and toes pointing skyward.

- Flexing from the hips (not the middle back), slowly lower your legs back toward your head. Keep your legs straight and locked at the knee throughout the movement. Keep your hands pressed in the small of your back to provide support.

- Now extend your arms out fully and clench your hands together. This will help counterbalance your legs. Lower your legs over your head so your toes are touching the floor. Keep your back straight and upright throughout this movement.

- Hold the pose for three breaths. You will feel a stretch in your hamstring muscles and around your shoulders and neck. Now relax your back and lower the knees toward your head. Unclench your hands and bring them off the floor and in toward your body.

■ exhale ▶ inhale ▶ inhale ॥

● Relax your knees and rest them against your forehead. Hold the *asana* for a minute—your breath may be shallow in this pose so do not try to breathe deeply. You will feel a stretch in your lower back.

● Now press your lower back toward the floor while keeping your knees in tight to your chest. Lower your feet toward your buttocks, flexing at the knees. Bring your hands up to your knees and hug them into your body briefly.

● Release the hug and lower your knees, bringing your hands away from your legs. Extend your legs out fully to recline on the floor.

● Lie full length on the floor, with your arms at your sides and the palms of your hands facing down. Relax and breathe deeply.

exhale ▶ **inhale** ▶ **exhale** ▶ ■

fish

matsyasana

This *asana* stretches the neck and upper and middle back; expands the chest; and increases circulation to the spine and brain; stimulating the thyroid, pituitary, and pineal glands. Perform the central stretch of the spine slowly and carefully—don't push beyond your natural limit. Breathing deeply while you are in this *asana* will enhance the effect of the stretch.

- Lie on your back with your legs fully extended, your feet together; and your arms flat at your side with the palms facing down. (For an easier lift, you can perform this exercise starting with your knees raised.)

- Slowly, begin to raise your head from the floor, lifting from the back and using your hands for balance. As you lift yourself higher, place your hands beneath your buttocks, palms flat against the floor.

- Lift your shoulders, and using your hands for support, bring yourself up on to your elbows, tucking them under your body as you lift. Keep your legs extended with toes pointing forward.

- Expand your chest slowly and continue to raise yourself, keeping your buttocks and legs flat on the floor. Roll your head backward and point your chin at the sky.

inhale ▶ begin to exhale ▶ exhale ▶

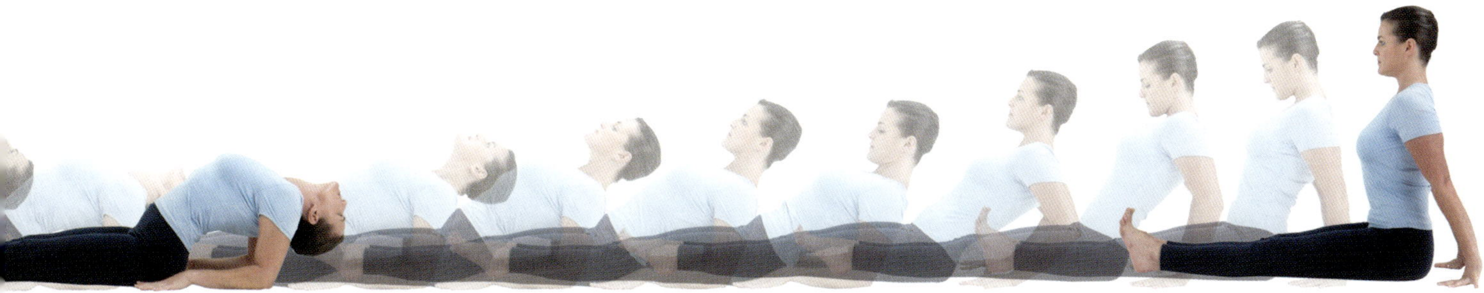

● Now push your chest out and roll your head back as far as you can without causing discomfort. Arch your spine inward. Hold this pose for three to six breaths. You will feel a stretch in your throat and chest.

● Release the stretch and slowly raise your head up to straighten your spine, lifting from the abdomen. Raise your body onto your elbows first, then lift upward using your hands. Keep your legs fully extended and flat on the floor throughout the movement.

● Continue to lift your chest forward using your hands. Bring your body fully upright to face forward, straightening your arms to lock at the elbows.

● Finish the sequence sitting upright in the *Dandasana* position (see pages 72–73), with your legs extended, back straight, and fingers resting on the floor behind to provide support.

inhale II **exhale** **inhale** ▶ **exhale** ▶ ■

yoga seal (1)

yogamudrasana

This sequence helps loosen the spine and shoulders. The movement continues onto the next page with a forward bend. In the full posture the feet are placed in *Padmasana*, the Lotus position. Here, it is sufficient to cross the legs.

- Sit upright on the floor in the *Dandasana* position (see pages 72–73), with your legs extended, back straight, and fingers resting on the floor behind to provide support.
- Keeping your back straight, lift up your left knee while at the same time bringing your right knee out to face 90 degrees from your body.
- Use your right hand to tuck your right ankle under your left thigh to rest behind the knee joint. Bring your left foot back in toward your body to cross your legs.
- Press both ankles down into the ground, maintaining a straight back and keeping your head upright. Your legs should be close into your body but comfortable. Rest both hands on the outside of your knees.

inhale ▸ exhale ▸ inhale ▸

Now lift both your hands away from your knees, extending out from the elbows. Maintain a straight spine throughout the movement.

Bring your hands behind your back and link your hands together, interlacing your fingers. Keep your shoulders down and do not hunch them toward your ears.

Extend your elbows and lock your arms, reaching out at an angle of roughly 45 degrees from the body. Lift your head up and stretch your throat.

Hold the pose for at least eight breaths, breathing from the lower abdomen. You will feel a stretch between your shoulders. Now continue the movement on the next page with the forward bend.

exhale ▶ **inhale** ▶ **exhale** ▶ **II**

yoga seal (2)

yoga mudrasana

This movement continues from the previous page with a forward bend with arms raised. This *asana* is counterbalanced with a back bend on the following pages.

- This sequence continues from the previous page. Keeping your arms extended and your hands clasped behind your back, begin to slowly lean your upper body forward.

- Bend forward from the hips, keeping your arms extended throughout the movement. Your spine should remain straight from the base to the neck.

- Continue to bend forward, at the same time lifting your arms higher as you bend. Remember to keep your extended arms locked and straight throughout to maximize the stretch.

- Lift your clasped hands as high as you can, remembering to keep your shoulders down and away from your ears. Tilt your head down to bring your forehead as close to the floor as is comfortable for you.

exhale ▸ **inhale** ▸ **exhale** ▸

● Hold this pose for three breaths. You will feel an intense stretch between the shoulder blades and along the length of the spine.

● Now gently lift your head from the floor to straighten your spine. Raise your body from the forward bend, keeping your arms straight, hands clenched, and elbows locked throughout the movement.

● Continue raising your body, hinging from the hips and keeping your spine straight. As you become upright, relax your arms at the shoulders and bring them in toward your body.

● Unclench your hands and bring them down to your sides. Straighten your body and return to an upright, seated posture.

inhale II **exhale** **inhale** ▶ **exhale** ▶ II

yoga seal (3)

yogamudrasana

This sequence begins with a back bend to counterbalance the forward bend on the previous spread, before finishing with the classic meditation *asana* with thumb and index finger joined.

- This sequence continues from the previous page. Sitting upright with legs crossed and your spine upright, walk your fingers back and away from the body until they are roughly eight inches away from your buttocks.

- Now slowly tilt your body backward, taking the weight on your arms as your extend the bend. At this point, keep your head facing upright.

- Continue to lean backward until the palms of your hands are resting flat on the floor. Your fingers should be pointing forward, roughly in the direction of your body.

- Once your body weight is fully supported on your arms, push your chest out and gently roll your head backward to point your chin at the sky. Hold the pose for three to six breaths. You will feel a stretch in your throat, abdomen, and chest.

inhale exhale inhale exhale

- Release the stretch and bring your head and upper body upright, hinging from the hips. As your body rises, bring your hands away from the floor and up onto your fingertips.

- Sit fully upright, with your spine straight from the base to the neck. Bring your hands out from your sides and rotate them around your body in a graceful, sweeping motion to come together in front of your chest.

- Now rest each hand on its respective knee, with the palms facing out. Join the thumb and index finger of each hand together to form circles, with your other three fingers pointed away from the body.

- Tilt your chin down and relax your whole body. Close your eyes and breathe slowly and deeply. You are now in a variation of the classic meditation *asana*, the Lotus position. If you wish, you can meditate.

inhale ▸ **exhale** ▸ **inhale** ▸ **exhale and relax** ■

advanced

reclining corpse

savasana

Although this *asana* looks very easy to perform, it is actually one of the hardest to master as the mind needs to stay present while the body relaxes and lets go. *Savasana* should be practiced for at least five minutes at the end of every yoga session.

● Begin the sequence in the Lotus position, sitting cross-legged and upright with your hands resting on your knees and the thumbs and index fingers of both hands joined.

● Gently lean your upper body backward and release your feet from under your body. Place your hands on the floor to support your body weight as you recline. Bring your knees and ankles together to align your legs.

● Lower your body back toward the floor, while at the same time taking your legs away from the center and extending them out in front of you. Support your weight on your arms throughout the movement.

● Slide your feet along the floor to extend them to a full stretch. Continue to lean back until your back is flat against the floor. Finally, lower your head so you are in a fully reclining position.

inhale ▶ **exhale** ▶ **inhale** ▶

Lie with your legs extended and your ankles a few inches apart. Your legs should be relaxed and your feet falling to the sides. Rest your arms at your sides, away from the body, and with your hands open and palms facing up toward the sky.

Now relax your muscles one by one, beginning with your facial muscles, then moving on to your neck, shoulders, arms, and legs until you feel calm and loose from head to toe.

Deepen your breathing to achieve a deep state of relaxation. You may want to listen to a relaxation tape, or cover your eyes to deepen the meditation. Stay in this *asana* for at least five minutes.

When coming out of *Savasana*, deepen your breathing. Each inhalation fills your body with energy and helps the waking process.

exhale

perfect posture

siddhasana

Siddhasana, or the Perfect Posture, involves placing one heel in front of the other. It employs the Lotus hand *mudra*. It is an excellent posture for practising meditation.

- The lotus flower is a significant symbol in Indian culture: although the plant has its roots in the mud, the flower constantly strives to lift its head toward the light of the sun.

- To take up the meditation *asana*, sit upright with the right leg inside the left leg and both legs pressed flat on the floor. Your spine should be upright, and your body should be relaxed.

- Bring the heels of your palms together, cupping your hands with your little fingers and thumbs touching. The fingers should be slightly bent to resemble the petals of a lotus flower.

- You are now ready to meditate. Hold the pose while keeping your back straight and your muscles relaxed. Your spine should be straight from the base up to the neck.

● Occasionally change the leg position by placing the left foot inside the right foot to develop the leg muscles evenly and to avoid cramping.

● Keep your breathing slow and deep. Practice the three-part breathing (see pages 14–15). Relax and breathe into the three positions of *Pranayama*, feeling a wave of breath move up and down your torso, from the lower belly up to the throat.

● Continue to practice rhythmic breathing until your mind is empty and you have achieved a deep state of relaxation. Meditate for 10 minutes.

● Advanced yoga practitioners can try sitting in the full Lotus if comfortable. This classic pose involves resting the backs of both feet high up on the opposing thighs and requires great flexibility in the legs and hips.

exhale ▶ **inhale** ▶ **exhale** II

glossary and suggested reading

Anga—A limb.

Ahimsa—This refers to the principle of non-violence, which is an essential tenet of many Indian religions such as Hinduism and Jainism.

Asana—This means posture, or "to sit in steadiness."

Astanga—This refers to the eight limbs of hatha yoga.

Bhagavad Gita—The mystical poem of Krishna is the kernel of the Hindu epic, *The Mahabharatha*.

Bhakti—The heart. It also means devotion to something.

Chakra—A vortex, or wheel of energy, situated in the body along the spine and in the head. There are seven chakras.

Dharana—This means concentration, especially when meditating or performing yoga.

Dhyana—This means meditation.

Guna—An attribute or quality. Three gunas compose the universe: raja, sattva, and tamas.

Guru—A spiritual teacher or "light dispeller."

Hatha—A yoga system that uses bodily techniques to train and still the mind.

Jnana—Knowledge or wisdom. Jnana yoga is the yoga of wisdom.

Karma—The universal law of cause and effect. It is also the yoga of action, work, and unconditional service.

Kundalini—Latent inner energy, represented by a coiled serpent of a feminine nature, which symbolically lies sleeping at the base of the spine. Yoga awakens this creative essence.

Mudra—Means "to delight in," a gesture, to concentrate energy.

Namaste mudra—The universal prayer position, commonly known and practiced in most of the world's major religions.

Nadi—A subtle energy line, like the meridian in Chinese medicine, in the body.

Niyama—Observances and discipline of the body.

Om—The sacred syllable, often used as a mantra in meditation practice.

Patanjali—An ancient sage who crystallized the eight limbs of yoga.

Prana—A subtle life-force.

Pranayama—The science of breathing.

Pratyahara—The withdrawal of the senses.

Raja—The royal path of yoga.

Rajas—This means unripeness, and is one of the three gunas (qualities).

Rishi—A seer or sage.

Sadhana—A spiritual path.

Saddhu—A holy man or ascetic who practices spiritual disciplines such as meditation and abstains from worldly pleasures.

Sannyassin—Someone who has given up all earthly things.

Samskara—Negative patterns of mental conditioning.

Sattva—The guna (quality) of purity, succulence, and balance.

Suryanamaskara—Meaning "salute to the sun," this is a sequence of flowing asanas.

Sutra—Sanskrit sayings, meaning a "thread of wisdom."

Swami—An Indian monk.

Tamas—The guna (quality) of inertia and over-ripeness.

Tapas—Meaning heat; intense discipline.

Upanishads—The spiritual writings of ancient Indian philosophy, exploring the link between the individual soul (Atman) with the universal soul (Brahman).

Vinyasa—This refers to breath-synchronized movement.

Yama—The first limb of yoga: restraints and rules of conduct.

Yogi—Male practitioner of yoga.

Yogini—Female practitioner of yoga.

Suggested reading

Tha Bhagavad Gita,
Translated by Juan Mascaro, Penguin Classics, 1962

How To Know God (*The Yoga sutra of Patanjali*),
commentary by Swami Prabhavananda and Christopher Isherwood, Vedanta Press, 1953

Light On Yoga,
B.K.S. Iyengar, Aquarian/Thorsons, 1991

The Heart Of Yoga,
T.K.V. Desijachar, Inner Traditions, 1995

Yoga for Life: How to Find the Right Style of Hatha Yoga,
Liz Lark, Carlton Books, 2001

Astanga Yoga: The Method of Breath-synchronised Movement Yoga,
Liz Lark, Carlton Books, 2000

index

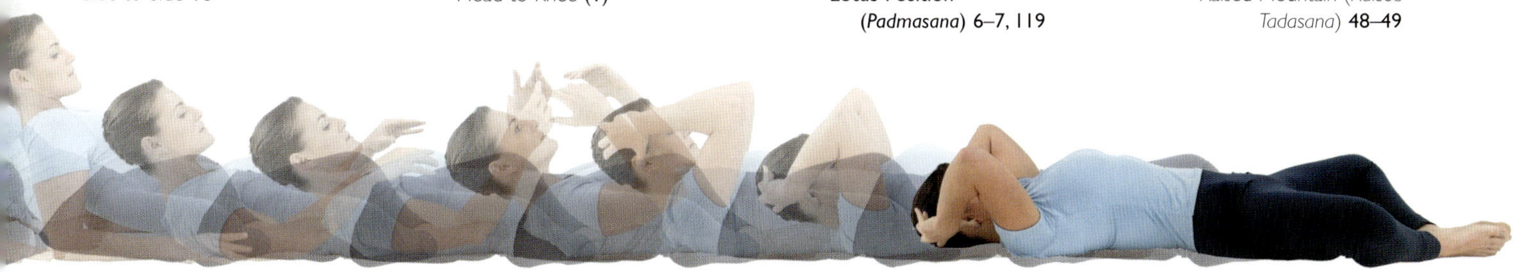